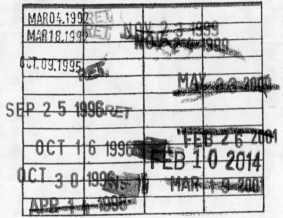

DATE DUE

MAR 04 1992	NOV 2 3 1999	
MAR 18 1993	NOV 1999	
OCT 09 1995		
	MAY 2000	
SEP 2 5 1996		
OCT 1 6 1996	FEB 2 6 2001	
OCT 3 0 1996	FEB 1 0 2014	
APR 1 1999	MAR 1 9 2001	

One Hundred Years of
Korean-American Relations,
1882–1982

One Hundred Years of Korean-American Relations, 1882–1982

Edited by

Yur-Bok Lee and Wayne Patterson

The University of Alabama Press

Library of Congress Cataloging in Publication Data

Main entry under title:

One hundred years of Korean-American relations, 1882–
1982.

Based on papers presented at the annual meeting of
the American Historical Association or that of the
Association for Asian Studies in 1982.
Bibliography: p.
Includes index.
1. United States—Foreign relations—Korea—
Congresses.   2. Korea—Foreign relations—United
States—Congresses.   I. Lee, Yur-Bok, 1934–.
II. Patterson, Wayne.
E183.8.K7056   1985   327.730519   84–24040
ISBN 0–8173–0265–4

To
Ae-Hyung
and
Marlene

Contents

viii

Contents

Preface

This book is based on extensive revisions of selected papers and discussions presented by members of the panels "One Hundred Years of Korean-American Relations, 1882–1982," at two academic conventions: the Annual Meeting of the American Historical Association (December 28, 1982, in Washington, D.C.) and the Annual Meeting of the Association for Asian Studies (April 3, 1982, in Chicago, Illinois). Both panels were organized to commemorate the centennial anniversary of the commencement of Korean-American relations, which occurred in 1882 upon conclusion of the Korean-American (Shufeldt or Chemulp'o) Treaty. The AHA panel was cosponsored by the Society for Historians of American Foreign Relations. In addition to Wayne Patterson and Yur-Bok Lee, Fred Harvey Harrington was also a member of both panels.

One of the editors (Wayne Patterson), who served as the chairperson of the AHA panel and a discussant of the AAS panel, and Hilary Conroy, who served as the commentator of the AHA panel, jointly provide chapter 1. In it, they not only comment on the contributions of the other five chapters but also elucidate the common themes of the authors of this book with an all-encompassing perspective, enabling readers to comprehend the unity of the period.

Chapter 2, contributed by the other editor (Yur-Bok Lee), examines Korean-American relations between 1882 and 1905 from the viewpoint of Korea as well as that of the United States, with due emphasis on the diplomatic role played by King Kojong (emperor, 1897–1907). Fred Harvey Harrington, one of the pioneers in the study of American policy toward the late Yi Dynasty of Korea, analyzes Korean-American relations for the

same period from the standpoint of American expansionism
and also of American domestic conditions (chapter 3). Wi Jo
Kang inquires into the delicate relations between the American
missionaries and the Japanese colonial government in Korea
after the Peninsula Kingdom became a part of the Japanese
Empire in 1905 (chapter 4). Robert T. Oliver, an illustrious adviser to the legendary Syngman Rhee (Yi Sŭng-man), offers
highly interpretive observations on Korean-American relations
during the 1940s and the 1950s (chapter 5). In chapter 6, Tae-
Hwan Kwak and Wayne Patterson explain why the United
States has been and is committed to maintaining the status quo
in the Korean peninsula.

For romanization systems throughout this book, we have
used McCune-Reischauer for the Korean, Wade-Giles for the
Chinese, and Hepburn for the Japanese. Some exceptions have
been made for well-known names (such as Syngman Rhee) and
places (such as Seoul, Tokyo, and Peking).

Grateful acknowledgment is due to Andrew C. Nahm and to
another anonymous reader, who read the entire manuscript and
made valuable comments for improvement of the study. We
would like to express our sincere gratitude to Curtis A. Amlund
and Lawrence H. Starkey for reading portions of this work and
for making numerous editorial and stylistic suggestions for its
betterment. The editors are also thankful to Ae-Hyung Lee (the
wife of the senior editor) for typing the final draft of the
manuscript.

It is our deep-felt hope that this volume will stimulate further
interest in Korean-American studies within the larger context
of East-West relations among American and Korean students.

Yur-Bok Lee
Wayne Patterson

One Hundred Years of
Korean-American Relations,
1882–1982

1

Duality and Dominance: A Century of Korean-American Relations

Wayne Patterson and Hilary Conroy

The centennial of Korean-American relations was manifested by a number of academic meetings in Korea and the United States, convened for the purpose of characterizing where the relationship has been, where it is, and where it is heading. As noted in the Preface, the chapters in this volume represent the findings of two of these meetings. They show the relationship to be a complex one, with disappointments and triumphs on both sides. In each of the following chapters the themes of duality and dominance appear, either implicitly or explicitly, and constitute a unifying element in this complex century-long relationship.

One need not look far to observe that there is a certain duality in the contemporary situation. After all, there are two Korean regimes, mutually hostile, with differing ideologies, economic structures, and alliance patterns. It is natural that from this division (caused in part by the United States) flow two radically different perspectives of a century of Korean-American relations. On the one hand, the South Korean government tends to characterize the relationship as one of equal partnership, where both sides share identical aims and problems are virtually nonexistent.

On the other hand, the North Korean government tends to characterize the relationship in extremely negative terms:

> The U.S. imperialists and the South Korean puppets are staging a farce to embellish the history of 100 years following the conclusion of the Korea-U.S. treaty as a history of friendship and cooperation. This is a most shameless fabrication of history and an intolerable insult to the Korean people. . . . The 100-year history of Korea-U.S. relations since the conclusion of the treaty has been a bloody period marked by incidents of aggression, marauding and homicide committed by the U.S. imperialists and a bitter history of shame and suffering for the Korean people.[1]

As historians dealing with the relationship between two nations, we are naturally skeptical of overly simplistic characterizations. Yet these two opposing views of the relationship capture at least one essence of the duality which began one hundred years ago, which exists to a lesser extent today and bids fair to persist for the foreseeable future.

There is bound to be a certain amount of duality in any bilateral relationship where two nations represent two different sets of interests. This is only natural and is to be expected. Problems arise only when one of the parties fails to recognize the divergence of interests. Most nations had by the late nineteenth century become sophisticated enough to make this distinction, but Korea possessed the naiveté of an innocent in the sometimes nefarious international politics of the age of imperialism. Yur-Bok Lee's essay, "Korean-American Diplomatic Relations, 1882–1905," goes to the heart of this problem by examining the failure of the Koreans to appreciate the fact that the 1882 treaty with the United States meant one thing to the Koreans and quite another to the Americans.

It was perhaps natural for Korea to rely too heavily on the letter of the treaty which promised good offices and, along with that, the hope that American advisers and diplomatic protection would come to the aid of a modernizing Korea, threatened by aggressive larger neighbors. After all, Korea had depended upon the Chinese for centuries, and it can be argued that dependence upon an outside power was not an unnatural response in Korea's foreign policy repertoire. Dependence may even have served Korea well, as long as the Chinese were willing and able to be depended upon. When China was no longer "dependable," after its defeat at the hands of Japan in 1895, Russia, Japan, and the United States appeared likely replacements. To the Koreans, Japan and Russia could not be trusted because they threatened Korean independence. Only the Americans could be trusted not to colonize Korea.

Korea needed the United States to intervene, but not to dominate. When the United States did little during the Sino-Japanese War (besides urge the end of hostilities), the Koreans should have taken a cue: the United States was not prepared to intervene in Korea. Ever since the United States established formal relations with Korea, America had been content to allow the dominant power in the region to take the lead. It had first been China, through whose offices American diplomats passed to open relations with Korea in 1882. When the Chinese were removed, the United States simply sat back and waited for the appearance of the next dominant power (in this case Japan) and prepared to follow its lead as well. At an early stage, the Americans had concluded that their interests in Korea were minimal and that it would be better to allow others to take the lead. After all, the United States allowed England to do the same in China for sixty years after the Opium War, and the United States derived great benefits from that relationship.

Unfortunately, the Americans spoke with two voices, not one, which began the duality which characterizes the relationship. The early phase of this relationship is familiar territory for Professor Lee of North Dakota State University. His *Diplomatic*

Relations between the United States and Korea, 1866–1887 and *Establishment of a Korean Legation in the United States, 1887–1890: A Study of Conflict between Confucian World Order and Modern International R~lations* are two of the guideposts in the historiography of this period. Moreover, because of Korean inexperience a pattern of dominance was begun in which Koreans reacted to American signals. That the Koreans tended to depend upon the wrong signals—in this case the written word of the treaty and the unofficial voices of American diplomats, to the detriment of official American policy— was tragic, for Korea believed the United States to be a friend, although official American policy was decidedly equivocal (at best) toward Korea's fate.

Why American policy, which had begun on a friendly and forward basis, became disinterested and uncaring is the theme of President Emeritus Fred Harvey Harrington of the University of Wisconsin, whose essay, "An American View of Korean-American Relations, 1882–1905," forms chapter 3 of this volume. His essay also deals with the frustrations of American diplomats, stationed in Korea, who lamented the lack of a more aggressive American policy and who came to champion the cause of Korea. Thus for Koreans, the shift in American policy may have been less noticeable because many American diplomats disagreed with official policy and continued to deal with the Korean activists, giving Koreans false hope in the process. In the end, it helps explain why Koreans continued to believe that the United States was prepared to take active measure to safeguard the independence of Korea.

It might well be argued that this aspect of duality in Korean-American relations is nothing more than a case of misunderstanding, as a result of a whimsical American policy, a few overzealous diplomats, and a Korean foreign policy that was oriented toward dependence and naive trust. But at least one diplomat, Horace Allen, was willing to use that duality to put one over on the Koreans. Allen, who is the subject of Professor Harrington's classic study, *God, Mammon, and the Japanese: Dr. Horace N. Allen and Korean-American Relations, 1884–1905*, took advantage of the overreliance of the Koreans on the United States and worked it to his own advantage. In one instance, he persuaded the Korean emperor to grant an emigration franchise to a friend (to pay off a political debt) by falsely stating that his friend was an official of the American government and that, by giving him the franchise, the emperor would strengthen ties between Korea and the U.S. government. And Allen did this knowing that neither the State Department nor the Korean emperor would be the wiser. So if Americans in official capacities were not above taking advantage of Korean ignorance and American power, we must conclude that this is a kind of domination which a friend would not expect of another friend, though it might not qualify as out-and-out imperialism.

When the Russo-Japanese War broke out, the Koreans hoped that the United States would intervene. Official policy suggested otherwise, and thus there was no American intervention. On the one hand, it may be argued that the United States should have intervened. From the Korean perspective, the result of the war would probably have been colonialism of one sort or another, no matter who won. American intervention, at worst, would be American colonialism and, at best, independence for Korea. On the other hand, had the United States intervened, there is no reason to expect that Korea would have fared any better than the Philippines, following the Spanish-American War of seven years earlier.

At any rate, when Japan moved toward making Korea a protectorate during and after the Russo-Japanese War, the Americans stood aside. President Roosevelt seemingly confirmed the leading role of Japan in Korea by approving the Taft-Katsura Agreement of 1905. In that year, Korea finally realized that the pro-Japanese Roosevelt would be no help in removing the protectorate and sent a secret delegation to the Hague Conference, to no avail. Thus with the United States (as well as the rest of the world) turning a deaf ear, the way was clear for Japan to annex Korea in 1910. Korea was swallowed up, into the Japanese empire, until the end of the Second World War.

Creation of the protectorate in 1905 and annexation in 1910 were responsible for the rise of Korean nationalism. Within Korea, a "righteous army" unsuccessfully fought the Japanese in the hills. Overseas, Koreans in Manchuria and the United States assassinated Itō Hirobumi and Durham White Stevens in expressions of outrage.

Ironically, this nationalist movement, which called for the liberation of Korea from Japanese rule, looked toward the United States. One of the leading and controversial figures in Korean nationalism, Syngman Rhee, had become Woodrow Wilson's protégé at Princeton. Later, Wilson's Fourteen Points, which called specifically for self-determination, gave Korean nationalists hope. Unfortunately, the duality in the relationship interfered. Wilson meant self-determination for countries which had been colonized by the Germans, but self-determination apparently did not apply to the colonies of friends, and Japan, after all, had been allied with the United States during World War I. The Koreans discovered this to their dismay when they (again secretly) sent a delegation to the Versailles Peace Conference, hoping for independence.

Domestically within Korea, the nationalist movement in the same year, 1919, exploded in the March First movement. It is no secret that many American missionaries were advocates of Korean independence, but they did not speak with the force of the American government behind them. Most treatments of Korean-American relations tend to ignore the colonial period because there were no government-to-government relations. Yet the essay by Wi Jo Kang, professor of World Religions and Mission at Wartburg Theological Seminary and an expert on religion during the Japanese colonial period, is important because relations need not be purely diplomatic. Moreover, even though the nature of the relationship differed in the 1910 to 1945 period, the same themes of duality and dominance again surface in his treatment of the subject.

In chapter 4 of this volume, "Relations between the Japanese Colonial Government and the American Missionary Community in Korea, 1905–1945," Professor Kang demonstrates the contrast between the "realist" policy of President Theodore Roosevelt, which was content to allow Japan to seize Korea for balance-of-power reasons, and the "idealistic" community of American missionaries, which in general sided with the Koreans against the often harsh aspects of Japanese colonial rule. The duality between realism and idealism occurred again in the failure at the Versailles Peace Conference.

A third (and final) example of the contrasting duality in the relationship can be noted in the private versus the public support for Korea during the colonial period. Although the U.S. government did not support Korean independence until World War II, an overwhelming majority of newspaper editorials in the United States tended to support Korea as a victim of Japanese imperialism.

Thus Wilsonian idealism, missionary support, and American public opinion stood in sharp contrast to government policy, which did not "come around" until Pearl Harbor. The fact that it was not until World War II that the United States supported Korea lends credence to the view that this support came only because it coincided with the interests of the United States.

While the United States was a Johnny-come-lately to the cause of Korean nationalism, the Soviets and the Chinese opposed the Japanese and supported the Koreans and Korean nationalists to a greater extent than the United States had. This led, at least in part, to divided loyalties among Koreans when liberation came, after thirty-five years of colonial rule. The

United States, which had not opposed Japan in Korea, began by relying on the Japanese in Korea during the early months of the occupation. By contrast, the Soviet Union (in the north) did not. It is hardly surprising, then, that many Koreans, perhaps still hoping to depend on a stronger foreign power, began to look to the Soviet Union and the Communist bloc for support after the war.

For the United States, though, the Pacific War and the Cold War which followed gave Korea an importance it had previously lacked. While there were voices which resisted the trend to place importance on the security of Korea, others argued that Korea was vital to American interests; and it is this latter theme that appears in chapter 5. Robert T. Oliver's essay, "Transition and Continuity in American-Korean Relations in the Postwar Period," examines these themes. An adviser to the first president of South Korea, Professor Oliver was in a unique position to observe events, and he has produced some interesting studies on Korea and President Syngman Rhee.[2] Scholar-diplomat Oliver asserts that the United States in the early postwar years did not recognize the Communist threat to Korea, as Syngman Rhee did, and that this lack of perception was only the beginning of a lack of understanding of things Korean on the part of the United States. Others argue that we did indeed perceive the threat of communism in Korea and, in response, imposed a postwar Korean society of our liking in the South.

No matter what view one holds on this subject, the Korean War increased American involvement to a level unprecedented in the century-old relationship with Korea. Thus while North Korea tended to depend on the Soviet Union and (later) China, South Korea tended to depend on the United States and (later) Japan, despite disappointments from earlier decades. At first, this support was primarily military (and perhaps still is), but U.S. support in the South also had political overtones. We supported the regime of Syngman Rhee in the South (1948–60) and sent massive amounts of economic aid after the end of the Korean War.

The relationship, however (as Professor Oliver demonstrates), was a troubled partnership. As the Rhee regime became increasingly corrupt and authoritarian, the United States faced a dilemma. When demonstrations broke out in the spring of 1960, the American refusal to back Rhee allowed his government to fall and be replaced by the Chang Myŏn regime, which lasted only one year. It was apparent that the United States in this instance was a catalyst for a more democratic political order. But it also led many Koreans again to rely on the United States in subsequent years, hoping the United States would (and could) stand up as the spokesperson for democracy. But Korea, now a growing economic power, became less politically dependent upon the United States after the military coup of Park Chung-hee in 1961. The United States officially deplored the military coup, which ended democracy in Korea, but was unable to prevent it. The most the United States could do was force elections in 1963, which transformed the military government into a civilian one.

It is in this context that chapter 6 looks at the current period in Korean-American relations. It is coauthored by Tae-Hwan Kwak of Eastern Kentucky University, a specialist on contemporary Korean politics and unification strategies, and is titled "The Security Relationship between Korea and the United States, 1960–1984." This essay argues that the security interest has become paramount in the relationship, as well as part of a basic American policy in Northeast Asia. This policy, which sought stability, identified stability as maintenance of the status quo. Practically, this policy of maintenance of the status quo means continuation of the division of Korea between North and South. Since moves toward reunification, even if peaceful, threaten the status quo and therefore stability, Koreans can expect little help from the United States in achieving reunifica-

tion. Just as considerations of a regional balance motivated
Theodore Roosevelt's actions at the turn of the century, a similar policy of maintaining a balance in East Asia has led successive American governments to support the government of
South Korea against North Korea in the name of stability.

While the relationship remains one-sided, this is not to say
that Korea is still a pawn. Its growing strength and importance
have transformed the duality in the relationship, to a point
where it is no longer completely one-sided. For example, the
Koreans like to portray themselves as loyal allies and friends of
the United States, grateful for the American troops and the
largess of economic and military aid, yet Korea has often not
behaved as a friend should. The United States has been willing
to overlook many excesses of its South Korean ally in its quest
for stability in Northeast Asia, but it does so in a somewhat
embarrassed way. Thus the United States finds itself at times on
the "receiving" end.

On the other hand, many Koreans have felt that the United
States has not always and consistently acted as a dependable
and faithful ally—not even after 1945. Such shifting policies as
those of President Carter's zigzag on maintaining American
ground forces in South Korea have reminded them of Truman-
Acheson's lukewarm commitment to the defense of South
Korea, which was at least partly responsible for the Korean War
of 1950 to 1953. Many Koreans think it terribly ironic and inconsistent for the United States to divide the Korean peninsula
along the 38th parallel in 1945, then fail to unify the country,
refuse to train and equip South Korean troops (unlike the Soviets in North Korea), and withdraw its troops and phase out its
commitment in South Korea—then get reinvolved when the
North attacked the South and modernize the South Korean
forces (under Eisenhower, Kennedy, Johnson, and Nixon), then
cause anxiety about the reliability of the American commit-

ment (under Carter) and, finally, reassert a firm pledge for the security of their country (under Reagan).

Some learned Koreans also wonder why Tong Sun Park's (Pak Tong-sŏn's) bribery was fully investigated and exposed in the United States although the alleged extralegal lobbying of agents of South Africa, Taiwan, and Israel has not been properly handled. Thus some South Koreans harbor grave misgivings about the fairness, dependability, and worthiness of the United States as an ally. Although some of their questions and doubts may be legitimate, these gainsayers constitute a minority. The overwhelming majority of South Koreans have nothing but good will and trust for the United States.

It is always hazardous to predict the future, but if the second century of Korean-American relations is relatively unchanged from the first, it may be prudent to suggest that the relationship will continue to be marked by a duality in which policy proceeds in two directions. And despite the growth in importance of Korea, the relationship will still be marked by the dominance of the United States. The history of this second century will of course be written by historians of the future. We will be satisfied if the essays in this volume illuminate some of the major themes in the first century of Korean-American relations.

In the following chapter, Professor Lee explores (among other things) the one-sidedness of Korean-American relations between 1882 and 1905, employing an innovative topical approach to the issues that King Kojong and his people perceived as crucial to the survival of Korea as an independent political entity.

2

Korean-American Diplomatic Relations, 1882–1905

Yur-Bok Lee

Very few monarchs in modern world history have suffered such a turbulent, fast-changing, and tragic career as King Kojong of Korea. During his rule (1863–1907), his kingdom was transformed from an isolated and antiforeign country to an open one, which struggled to maintain its autonomy and political identity amid the harsh politics of both Western and Asian imperialism—only to lose its identity in 1905.

In 1863, the twelve-year-old boy became king of Korea and came to be known by his reign title Kojong, almost by accident.[1] Because of his youth, however, his strong-willed father, the Taewŏn'gun, was the real ruler until 1873, when Kojong reached adulthood and assumed personal rule. During the forty-four years of his reign, Korea drifted from an isolated "Hermit Kingdom" into a semimodern state by establishing treaty relations with Japan and the Western powers; enacted some modern reforms; became entangled in the power politics not only of neighboring countries like China, Japan, and Russia, but of faraway England and the United States; experienced the violent death of Queen Min; and then finally found itself absorbed by the Japanese.

Throughout these troubles and during his entire reign (especially after 1882), Kojong persistently sought American aid in trying to solve Korea's problems.[2] Thus why and how Kojong maintained great faith in the United States is very important in the study of Korean-American relations. Harrington argues from the American domestic perspective (in the next chapter) that U.S. policy toward Korea was inconsistent, indifferent, unconcerned, and thus hardly reliable, but emphasis in this chapter is placed on the issue of why Kojong expected so much from the United States in trying to modernize and free his kingdom first from Chinese control and later from Japanese domination, and why the United States, the first Western treaty power in Korean history, proved unwilling and unable to provide what Korea wished and needed so badly.

Sources of Kojong's Pro-American Attitude and Policy

To begin with, Kojong's ideology and pragmatism were important factors in his strong and persistent pro-American orientation. Although he remained a good Confucian ruler all his life, he became a surprisingly practical, flexible, and realistic ruler, especially in foreign matters.[3] In fact, conclusion of the Korean-Japanese (Kanghwa) Treaty of 1876 was possible partly because of his strong support for it.[4] Furthermore, even before final conclusion of another instrument, the Korean-American Treaty of 1882, Kojong had already become pro-American— ironically, because of the strong influence of the Chinese. In 1879, Viceroy Li Hung-chang of China had advised Yi Yu-wŏn, a Korean leader, that Korea should try to cope with the aggressive and ambitious nations of Japan and Russia by "opening" herself to friendly Western powers.[5] Apparently, Li's advice had an effect upon Kojong and his followers.

But the most important source of Kojong's favorable impression of the United States was a booklet, *Chao-hsien ts'e-lüeh* [A Policy for Korea]. This essay had been written by Huang Tsun-hsien, the counselor to the Chinese legation in Tokyo. In 1880, Huang and Ho Ju-chang, the Chinese minister in Tokyo, urged

Ambassador Kim Hong-jip, of the Korean mission to Japan, to take the booklet to Kojong. In it, Huang proposed that, in view of potential Russian threats, Korea should stimulate her "self-strengthening" by maintaining close ties with China and Japan, by adopting modernizing reforms, and by allying with the United States. In Huang's view, the United States, a powerful industrial and anti-imperialist power, was a moral state, founded upon Christianity, which usually supports weaker nations against strong oppressors. Fortunately (or perhaps unfortunately), Kojong was apparently convinced of Huang's naive perception of the United States;[6] and in due time this half-truthful misperception had a tremendous impact upon Kojong and his adherents. In short, it was partly because of his favorable idea about the United States that Kojong played such a positive role in "opening" Korea to the United States in 1882.

Another factor was the geographical distance between Korea and the United States. Kojong and many other Koreans believed that the United States, thousands of miles away across the Pacific, would have no evil or ulterior motives. If the United States had been close by, the Koreans would undoubtedly have had substantial misgivings about Americans. Also, Kojong placed strong trust in the United States because—unlike Great Britain and France, which, though far away, had colonies in Asia—the United States had no Asian colonies and had shown only commercial interest in Korea.[7]

Thus, possessing a favorable impression of the United States, Kojong was said to have "danced for joy" when Lucius H. Foote, the first American minister, arrived in Seoul in May 1883, as envoy extraordinary and minister plenipotentiary.[8] In his first audience with the king, Foote explained that, in negotiating the treaty, the United States was motivated largely by concern for "the comfort and happiness" of the Korean people, that "in this progressive age" there was a moral power "more potent than standing armies," and that "the weakness of a nation was some-

times its strength"—sentiments which corroborated Kojong's
faith in the United States.[9]

It is understandable, therefore, that Kojong and his reform-
minded advisers felt that their pro-American policy was justified by the friendly and benevolent attitudes displayed by American diplomatic agents in Korea. Beginning with Foote and continuing with George C. Foulk, Hugh Dinsmore, John M. B. Sill,
and Horace N. Allen, all American agents made substantial contributions to development of a friendly attitude by the Korean
government toward the United States.[10] Without being privy to
the thinking at the White House, the Department of State, and
the United States in general, Kojong and his pro-American advisers believed that the amicable attitudes of American diplomats in Seoul reflected the very essence of American policy.

A final reason why Kojong became and remained pro-American is the fact that in 1882, after the U.S. government had
become the first Western power to conclude a treaty with
Korea, the Korean-American Treaty served as the model for all
treaties between Korea and other Western powers. Consequently, the Korean-American Treaty of 1882 had a tremendous
psychological impact upon the Koreans. They thought that
whatever happened to their country after 1882 would be a con-
sequence of this treaty and that the United States, therefore,
had a moral obligation to them.

International Status of Korea to 1895

That the kingdom of Korea had been traditionally a dependency or tributary to China within the framework of an East
Asian world order is well known. But the question of when the
kingdom became sovereign and independent (in 1876 or 1882
or 1895?) within the modern concept of international relations
is the most controversial in the study of Korea's foreign rela-

tions during the last quarter of the nineteenth century. The conventional thesis is that, despite Korea's modern treaties with Japan in 1876 and Western powers in the early 1880s, Korea became independent only after China relinquished her claim to suzerainty over Korea following the Sino-Japanese War of 1894 and 1895.[11] That thesis, however, has been challenged and repudiated by recent scholarship. For example, Key-Hiuk Kim (in a recent study) insists that Korea was brought into the framework of the Western international system and was made independent, "at least partly," by the earlier Korean-Japanese Treaty of 1876.[12]

After 1882 the official position of the U.S. government was that Korea became sovereign and independent by the Korean-Japanese Treaty of 1876; that the United States signed the Korean-American Treaty of 1882 on the basis that Korea was a fully sovereign kingdom; and that therefore the United States was bound to treat Korea as a full-fledged, independent country.[13] The Japanese government also insisted that it had negotiated and concluded the Korean-Japanese Treaty of 1876 in the theory and belief that Korea was fully sovereign and independent.[14] Therefore, the Japanese government agreed with the American position.

The Chinese government, however, disagreed with the United States, insisting that though Korea was independent in her relations with treaty powers, in her relations with China she was still a dependency[15]—a position that was not only confusing but, in fact, incompatible with the modern system of international law and relations. To complicate matters further, the Chinese in reality attempted to dictate not only Korea's relations with themselves but her relations with the United States, Japan, and other treaty powers as well—and, in fact, even Korea's domestic affairs—as if Korea were their new colony.[16] Thus China, after 1882, created the most serious problem in Sino-Korean-American diplomatic relations.

Briefly, this is what happened to the status of Korea after 1876. Although the kingdom was brought into the framework of the modern international system and so became independent, at least in part, by the Korean-Japanese Treaty of 1876, the Korean leaders apparently failed to realize the full implications of the treaty and still acted as if Korea were a tributary to China. Of course, the Chinese leaders had no intention or desire to regard Korea as an independent nation on account of the Korean-Japanese Treaty.

After conclusion of the Korean-American Treaty of 1882, however, King Kojong decided to free his kingdom from Chinese domination and modernize his country with American aid. By then, the Ch'ing Dynasty had become so weakened and degenerate that Kojong felt he should distance his kingdom from China and ally it closely with the United States. In fact, he and his followers regarded the United States as the symbol of a benevolent power that would guarantee the integrity and independence of Korea, and they viewed the Korean-American Treaty as an instrument to free Korea from Chinese control. But the problem before 1894 was that the more Korea tried to escape from China, the more China tried to control Korea in the name of suzerain-dependency relations, but actually in the manner of a new and aggressive imperialism.

The Chinese appeal to traditional suzerain-dependency relations to justify their tight control of Korea was intended to give an air of historical legitimacy to the policy; but in actuality, the whole policy was misdirected and short sighted, because it eventually led to disaster following the Sino-Japanese War of 1894 and 1895. Since a politically stable and militarily and economically strong Korea would have undoubtedly served as a strong buffer between China and Japan, and therefore might have prevented the Sino-Japanese War, Li and the Manchu leaders should not have hampered Kojong's reform efforts and policies.

But Li and his contemporary Manchu and Chinese leaders were not far-sighted statesmen. Despite some reforms in connection with the Self-strengthening Movement, the Chinese leadership at that time did not have a clear-cut blueprint for making its country strong and stable. What it could not do for its own country, it certainly could not do for Korea.

Both the American government and its diplomats in Seoul deeply resented Chinese interference in the affairs of Korea. Many of these diplomats were deeply involved in the struggle for the independence of Korea and were strongly opposed to Chinese Resident Yüan Shih-k'ai's attempt to control Korean affairs. Nonetheless, so far as the U.S. Department of State was concerned, beyond obligating itself to deal with Korea as an independent nation, it never felt committed to ensure and guarantee the integrity and independence of Korea. In the words of Secretary of State Thomas Bayard: "The agitation of the subject of Corea's complete independence of China is neither desirable nor beneficial," inasmuch as the American interest in Korea was "merely the protection of American citizens and their commerce."[17]

Further confusing the already complex issue of the independence of Korea, King Kojong acted timidly. Rather than telling off the Chinese and urging that, since Korea had become independent, China not interfere in Korean affairs, he chose to deal with China in a seemingly diplomatic but timorous manner. Kojong repeatedly assured American diplomatic agents in Seoul that his kingdom was a sovereign and independent country; yet toward China he tried to show his independence by deed more than words. But whenever the Chinese intimidated and threatened him and his advisers, he backed down, only to reassert his sovereignty at the next possible opportunity.

For example, in a vitally important struggle for the independence of his kingdom vis-à-vis China in connection with establishment of permanent Korean legations in Japan, the United

States, and Europe in 1887, Kojong initially took bold action by sending a mission to Japan without consulting the Chinese in advance,[18] and he was about to do the same in establishing a legation in the United States.[19] But when China coerced him to send a memorial asking the Chinese emperor for permission for such a mission, the king humbly complied with the Chinese demand,[20] thus acting like a good, dependent king. In 1890 Kojong notified the Chinese emperor of the death of the dowager, his foster mother, and asked the emperor *not* to send a commission—officially, by reason of the great economic cost of such a commission, but in reality to undermine or weaken Korea's traditional ties with China. When the Chinese emperor sent the commission by ship, thereby saving Korea great expense, Kojong treated the commission with the highest respect as the emissary of the Chinese emperor.

Moreover, Kojong's attempt to free Korea from China was frequently complicated by his pro-Chinese ministers. For example, in 1887 Foreign Minister Kim Yun-sik told American Minister Dinsmore that Korea was a "truly independent kingdom and China is only our elder brother and because we are weak and a small country we ask China to advise and assist us."[21] Kim acted so often like a Chinese agent or puppet, rather than like the Korean foreign minister, that Kojong had to dismiss him.

Nevertheless, there is no clear evidence that Kojong tried to terminate all traditional ties with China. In fact, he did not mind retaining friendly relations with China. It should also be noted that even when China was seemingly oppressive of Korea in the 1880s and 1890s, the Korean government never formally invoked the good-offices clause of the Korean-American Treaty. All in all, therefore, Kojong wanted to maintain a loose tie with China, but to make his country more independent of Chinese influence and control, since China could no longer provide what Korea needed for regeneration. Also, he wanted the

United States not only to provide what Korea needed but to ensure or guarantee the independent status of Korea as a kind of new elder brother.

From the standpoint of the United States, this was the most puzzling legal question in Korean-American diplomatic relations at that time. The United States could ignore China's half-empty claim to suzerainty over Korea. After all, China had continuously claimed suzerainty over Ryūkyū and Annam as late as 1886, without asking whether the Japanese and French agreed. However, Korea's performance of ceremonies in accordance with the age-old suzerain-dependency relation, whether done forcefully or voluntarily, was an entirely different matter. But most important of all, the fact that Korea kept sending tributary missions to China until the Chinese were driven out of Korea in 1894 and 1895 is a strong indication that Korea did not become a full-fledged and completely independent country after 1876 and 1882.[22] The fact is that, until 1895, Korea's international status was dualistic: partly dependent and partly independent.

American Good Offices

As far as the U.S. government was concerned, probably the most important part of the Korean-American Treaty was the protection of American seamen and the opening of trade.[23] As far as the Korean government was concerned, however, the most important part of the treaty was the good-offices clause of article 1. It states that

> There shall be perpetual peace and friendship between the President of the United States and King of Chosen and the citizens and subjects of their respective governments. If another power deals injustly or oppressively with either Government, the other will exert their good offices, on being informed of the case, to bring about an amicable arrangement, thus showing their friendly feelings.[24]

Since the Revolutionary War, the independence and integrity of the United States has never been seriously threatened by Mexico, Canada, or Spain—or even by the British. In sharp contrast, the history and geopolitics of Korea have been troubled: the Peninsula Kingdom has been invaded and sacked by the Chinese, the Mongols, the Japanese, and the Manchus. In recent years, the Koreans have had minor wars even with French and American marines,[25] and have lived under the presumed threat of a Russian push from the north. In view of its military and political history and the fact that all its neighbors have been much bigger and more powerful than herself, it is very understandable that Korea sought an ally or protector who would willingly offer "good offices" in times of international crisis or distress.

Korea, accordingly, has repeatedly invoked this good-offices clause, sometimes too freely and unnecessarily; and the clause has precipitated serious controversy and misunderstanding between Korea and the United States. Indeed, some historians characterize this clause as "an act of absent-mindedness" on the part of the United States.[26] Actually, all the other treaties that Korea subsequently made with foreign powers also included the clause. To the Americans, the term *good offices* implied no special obligation; it was merely a sign of friendship, couched in the language of diplomatic nicety.[27] It meant that the United States would give moral and diplomatic support to the independence and integrity of Korea, but it never implied a commitment to or guarantee of physical protection of the sovereignty and independence of Korea.[28]

However, King Kojong and his adherents interpreted the good-offices provision to mean that the United States would guarantee the territorial integrity and political independence of Korea by taking sides with Korea in cases of foreign aggression or oppression. They sincerely believed that the American "guarantee" was not only a legal but a moral commitment.[29] Thus whenever they felt threatened or oppressed by powers other than China, they requested American "good offices." In 1885, when the British illegally occupied Port Hamilton (Kŏmundo), to use against Russia in case of an Anglo-Russian war on account of the Afghan crisis, the Korean government formally invoked the good-offices clause of the Korean-American Treaty. American Chargé George Foulk forwarded the Korean request to his government, but Secretary of State Bayard replied that the treaty neither empowered nor obligated the United States to interfere on behalf of Korea.[30]

On the eve of the Sino-Japanese War of 1894 and 1895 and during its course, the Korean government repeatedly asked the United States' "good offices" in preventing Japan from imposing her will on Korea.[31] Initially, Secretary of State Gresham and President Cleveland sympathized with Korea and tried to exert moral and diplomatic influence on the Japanese government; but that was all. Beyond sending strong diplomatic notes of the U.S. view to the Japanese government, they were not willing to go.[32] When the British asked whether the United States would be willing to join Britain, Russia, Germany, and France in an intervention on behalf of Korean independence, the United States rejected the suggestion. Cleveland and Gresham agreed that forceful intervention against Japan—whether unilateral, bilateral, or multilateral—would be contrary to the traditional American policy in Asia and that the negligible American economic and other interests in Korea would hardly warrant their administration's breaking of that tradition. They concluded that if Korean independence could be preserved only through American intervention, supported by military force, then it was to America's advantage that Korea be dominated by others. In fact, Gresham noted that the American policy was to avoid any alliance and embarrassing participation in guaranteeing the independence and integrity of distant states.

After the war, a Japanese-inspired plot in Seoul resulted in the murder of anti-Japanese Queen Min and the king's temporary domicile in the Russian legation as a refugee. American Minister Sill joined the representatives of Britain, Russia, and France in urging the Japanese to facilitate the king's return to his palace, but Secretary of State Olney reacted sharply, instructing Sill to confine himself to the protection of American citizens and not become embroiled in the internal affairs of Korea. Not only Olney, but none of his successors—neither John Sherman, William R. Day, nor John Hay—showed special interest in Korea.

In 1897, Sherman told the newly appointed minister, Allen, that he was not a "counselor" to the Korean government, that the U.S. government had no "protective alliance" with Korea, and that American citizens in Korea should maintain "absolute neutrality" in Korean affairs. Nevertheless, King Kojong, not knowing the thoughts of American secretaries of state and presidents, told Minister Allen in 1900 that "we feel that America is to us as our Elder Brother."[33]

The United States, after becoming a Far Eastern power by acquiring the Philippines in 1898, became very concerned with equal commercial opportunity in China. Thus, when the idea of the American Open Door policy was being discussed in Washington, Kojong asked Minister Allen to obtain the same policy for Korea. However, when Secretary of State Hay finally announced his Open Door policy in 1899 and 1900, Korea was not included.

After Great Britain signed the Anglo-Japanese Alliance of 1902, recognizing Japan's special interest in Korea and thereby indicating British willingness to allow Korean independence to be submerged under Japanese domination, the United States thought seriously about renegotiating its treaty with Korea along similar lines (but the Korean leaders were apparently not aware of this). On the eve of the Russo-Japanese War of 1904 and 1905, the Korean government correctly declared neutrality and maintained undue or unwarranted confidence in American "good offices."[34]

When the war broke out, Hay instructed Allen to do everything possible for the protection of American interests, consistent with absolute neutrality. As for President Roosevelt, he felt that Japan was playing an important role in the American interest by maintaining a balance of power in the area.[35] Thus he had to weigh the maintenance of Korean independence against the balance of power in East Asia. Consequently, he and Hay urged the belligerents to respect the Open Door policy in China, but said nothing about Korea. In actuality, however, as early as 1900 Roosevelt had concluded that Japan should have Korea as a check upon Russian expansion.[36]

Roosevelt's ideology and feelings played a significant role in his policy toward East Asia and the Russo-Japanese War; he was very pro-Japan and anti-Russia. As for Korea and the Koreans, he held a low opinion, influenced partly by the writings of George Kennan and Arthur J. Brown.[37] Thus he told Hay in January 1905: "We cannot possibly interfere for the Koreans against Japan. They could not strike one blow in their own defense."[38] During his presidency, Roosevelt held the view that Korea should come under the Japanese, although his administration officially kept neutral in the war. It should be noted that Roosevelt served as the mediator by offering the good offices of the United States for the conclusion of the war; for this service he was awarded a Nobel Peace Prize—at the sacrifice of Korea.[39]

In the summer of 1905 the Roosevelt administration signed the Taft-Katsura Memorandum, providing that Japan would respect American interests in the Philippines in return for American recognition of Japanese interests in Korea.[40] This controversial agreement can be seen as even more significant in light of the relationship between it and the Second Anglo-Japanese

Treaty and the Treaty of Portsmouth. In August 1905, about two months after the end of the war, the Japanese government finally made the Treaty of Protectorate with Korea.[41] Ten days later, the American government closed its legation in Seoul, terminating diplomatic relations.

Before and during the Russo-Japanese War, Kojong believed he might have little to fear from the hostilities, expecting that American "good offices" would protect Korean neutrality and independence. The Korean expectation, however, was far out of proportion to any Western legal concept of good offices. On the eve of the war, one of Kojong's confidants, Yi Yong-ik, told Frederick A. McKenzie, a Canadian journalist working for the *London* (England) *Daily News*, that since his country had "the promise of America," he expected the United States "to protect" Korea.[42] In April 1904, Minister Allen wrote to Secretary of State Root that the emperor of Korea expected that America would "do something . . . to retain for him as much of his independence as possible" and would interpret the good-offices clause of the treaty very freely; that he expected the United States to invoke the clause and use its "good offices" in the crisis.[43] Meanwhile Allen, because of strong disagreement with Roosevelt's pro-Japanese policy, was replaced by Minister Edwin V. Morgan, whose main mission in Korea was to close the American legation as smoothly and diplomatically as possible. Again, not realizing Morgan's real mission, Kojong appealed to him, since the Japanese were pressuring him to arrange a protocol by which they would assume external control of Korea.

Between September 1904 and December 1905, the Korean government made six appeals to the Roosevelt administration,[44] but all failed in the end. Secretary Root's handling of the fifth appeal may be taken as typical of American policies and attitudes toward Korea and Japan. In late October 1905, Kojong decided to make a direct appeal to Roosevelt through Homer B.

Hulbert, Kojong's confidant and American educator, in a secret mission. On November 15, Hulbert appeared at the Department of State in Washington with a letter from the Korean emperor to the president of the United States, but he was kept waiting outside Root's office for several days—until Korea, on November 17, had signed away to Japan its powers to conduct foreign relations.[45] Hulbert was then admitted and was told that the United States must deal with the emperor's protest through Japan, since the latter had legal control of Korea's foreign relations.[46] Root did not mention the fact that he had already ordered Minister Morgan to terminate diplomatic activities by closing the American legation.

On December 11 the emperor sent Hulbert a cable, stating that he had been forced to sign the so-called Treaty of Protection "at the point of a sword and under duress" and that therefore it was "null and void." The message was conveyed to Root by Minister Min Yŏng-ch'an, the Korean minister to France, then in the United States as a special envoy without credentials.[47] Root's reply was paradoxical. He explained that no country could utilize its good offices unless requested to do so by the government to which they have been promised, but that, since Korea's foreign relations were now handled by Japan, such a request could come only through a Japanese channel.[48] Roosevelt wholeheartedly backed Root's logic and handling of the whole matter.

Since the United States failed to respond favorably to his appeals, the Korean emperor dispatched a secret emissary to the Second International Peace Conference at The Hague in 1907. Furious, the Japanese retaliated by deposing him and forcing on Korea the Convention of July 24, 1907, which gave Japan control of many of Korea's internal governmental functions.[49] In 1910, when Japan finally annexed Korea, removing the five-year fiction of *de jure* independence,[50] the United States raised no objection (and was probably pleased).

American Military Advisers

The vitally important role that Westerners played in modernizing Japan and the positive responses that the Japanese leadership gave to what Western advisers and instructors offered for her modernization during the latter part of the nineteenth century comprise a well-known story.[51] As for China, on the other side, the frustrations, disappointments, difficulties, obstructions, evasions, and opposition that Westerners faced in attempting to help modernize her are probably equally well known.[52] Less well known—and often misunderstood—is how the Korean leadership reacted to the West's attempt to modernize its country. The story goes back thirty years earlier.

Following the conclusion and implementation of the Korean-Japanese Treaty of 1876, the reform-minded Kojong became interested in modernizing his troops and military organizations. Seventy Korean students were sent to China and fourteen to Japan for military training; in addition, eighty Korean soldiers were to be trained by a Japanese officer.[53] However, after the Soldiers' (*Imo*) Revolt of 1882 (an anti-Japanese and anti-reform revolt), Kojong became more cautious in his approach to reforms and authorized China to assume responsibility for a new program of military training.[54] Then, after the arrival of American Minister Foote, Kojong determined to hire American military instructors and asked Foote to help him. Foote responded favorably by conveying the message to Secretary of State Frelinghuysen.

At the same time that Kojong was conferring with Foote on American military instructors, the first Korean mission was in Washington, D.C., asking the U.S. government to send (among others) military and diplomatic advisers; and it received a favorable reply. Thus beginning in October 1883 (in response to requests from Kojong), Foote repeatedly asked his superiors in Washington to send American military and diplomatic advisers to Korea. In addition, since Admiral Shufeldt had previously expressed his willingness to the Korean mission in Washington to go to Korea as a military adviser, Foote (at the king's request) asked Shufeldt to "come at once"; but he did not.[55] After Foote's departure from Korea in 1885, Chargé Foulk, a strong advocate of the independence and modernization of Korea through American aid, repeated the king's requests for American advisers and urged the new Secretary of State, Bayard, to comply with the Korean wish.[56] But it was not until 1888, after five years of delay, that four American military advisers were sent to Korea.

The main reasons for such a delay were not only constitutional and bureaucratic impediments but also the lukewarm attitudes of the American officials. To begin with, Foote's initial dispatch to the secretary of state had been mislaid, which caused about one year's delay. Then there were legal and technical procedures, such as winning the approval of the secretary of war, the president, and above all Congress (as provided by Article 1, Section 9, of the U.S. Constitution).[57] Secretary Frelinghuysen, having eagerly supported the idea of opening Korea to the United States and having promised to send American advisers when the Korean mission was in Washington, was in favor of complying with the king's request. But neither his successor, Bayard, nor the commanding general of the army, Philip Sheridan, nor Congress was enthusiastic about sending American instructors to a faraway kingdom such as Korea.[58] Even after the secretaries of state and of war and the president himself approved the proposal, the measure had to be brought before the Senate, where it was referred to the Committee of Military Affairs; but no action was taken. It was not until 1887 that the proposal finally came alive through the suggestion of W. W. Rockhill, chargé d'affaires of the American legation in Seoul, who recommended that the officers be chosen from men who either had resigned from the armed forces or had not received commissions after graduating from the military academy.[59] (The king agreed to pay $5,000 [Mexican] to a chief military instructor and $3,000 to each of his two assistants, in addition to providing housing and travel expenses.)

In selection of the advisers, Commanding General of the Army Sheridan had a free hand. He chose William McEntyre Dye, one of his West Point classmates, as chief of the Korean Military Mission. Dye had adequate credentials, having served with distinction on the Western frontier and in the Civil War, and had been promoted to brigadier general of volunteers. After resignation from the army in 1870, Dye had served under the khedive of Egypt, then as superintendent of metropolitan police for the District of Columbia, and finally in the Bureau of Pensions.

Dye, in turn, was permitted to choose his own staff.[60] Unfortunately, two of the men he chose turned out to be unfit as military instructors in a strange and faraway country. His first assistant was Edmund H. Cummins, who had been a Confederate major and later a patrolman in the District of Columbia. In 1887, he was already sixty-four years old.[61] The second assistant was Dr. John Grigg Lee, age thirty. Educated in France, Dr. Lee became a physician, but he had no military experience beyond his membership in a Pennsylvania militia.[62]

These three officers arrived at Seoul in April 1888 and were soon joined by a fourth man, Ferdinand J. H. Nienstead, age thirty-five. Because of the long delay in the arrival of the American military instructors, the American consulate in Osaka, Japan, at the request of American Minister Dinsmore, sent Nienstead (who was vice-consul and translator in the American consulate at Kobe) to Korea. But Nienstead's military experience consisted of only one term of service, as a navy pay clerk.[63] Despite the sorry qualifications of these Americans (except Dye), Kojong and his reform-minded advisers were delighted with their arrival, and Dye, Cummins, Lee, and

Nienstead were made general, colonel, major, and captain respectively.

Among other things, these men were to train a nucleus of forty cadets, who in turn would develop a training program for a larger, modern Korean army. Almost as soon as they started the training program, however, Cummins and Lee became problems: they detested their job and Korea, neglected their duties, got drunk too often, griped about living conditions, quarreled with Nienstead, and complained of delinquency in payment of their salaries. Although some of their complaints, such as the payments, were justified, most of their complaints were intolerable to Dye and the Korean government. Thus on September 18, 1889, on the recommendation of Dye, the Korean government dismissed Cummins and Lee.[64]

With the dismissal of these two men, Kojong's idea of developing an officers' corps at the military training school turned into a disaster. Nienstead stayed in Korea a few more years, assisting Dye in training Korean soldiers.[65] As for Dye himself, he stayed in Korea until 1899, serving Kojong in various roles. Sustained by Kojong's strong confidence in him, Dye played an important role during and after the Sino-Japanese War of 1895.[66] But as early as 1893, Kojong, disappointed with the failure of his military modernization, thought of sending Korean cadets to the U.S. Naval Academy; he had to drop this idea, however, because of Chinese opposition.[67] After 1895, the Japanese played the dominant role even in Korean military training.

The important point in the fiasco of the first American military mission to Korea is the fact that the delay and careless selection of the American instructors, by American officials, symbolizes the one-sidedness of Korean-American relations before 1905: Korea's unfailing but unwarranted faith in the United States and the American government's lukewarm and reluctant participation in the modernization of a remote and tiny kingdom.

American Diplomatic, Civil, and Educational Advisers

The first Western diplomatic adviser to the Korean government was not an American but a German, P. G. von Möllendorff, presumably a close confidant of Viceroy Li. Li had manipulated the Korean government into asking him to select and send a foreign-affairs adviser to Korea in 1883,[68] and he had chosen von Möllendorff for two reasons: to check the growing Japanese influence and to further Chinese interests in Korea. Once in Korea, however, von Möllendorff, who was appointed vice-minister of the Foreign Office and inspector general of Korean customs, became *anti*-China and determined to promote the welfare and interests of Korea. Moreover, he wanted to separate Korea further from Chinese control, by allying her closely with Russia.[69]

Deeply disappointed with the American delay in sending military and other advisers, Kojong gave tacit approval to von Möllendorff's secret attempt to have Russia provide military instructors for Korea, in return for leasing Port Lazareff to the Russians. When the Chinese, Japanese, British, and Americans discovered von Möllendorff's move, all were strongly opposed to it and pressured the Korean government to dismiss him.[70] In the case of the United States, although the government itself was not agitated by von Möllendorff's idea of bringing Russia into Korea, American Chargé Foulk was so alarmed that he added his influence to the pressures for von Möllendorff's discharge.

After the dismissal, Li divided von Möllendorff's functions into two parts, making Judge Owen Nickerson Denny an adviser in foreign affairs and Henry F. Merrill the chief of the customs service. Kojong had reservations about Li's arbitrary way of selecting and sending foreign advisers to Korea, but he accepted them without formal protest, largely because they were Americans. During his four-year tenure in Korea, Merrill reformed the Korean maritime customs service and tripled its revenue, but unlike von Möllendorff, who had fought the Chinese to promote Korean interests, he remained loyal to Li and to Robert Hart (head of the Chinese maritime customs service) and served their interests at the expense of Korea.

Judge Denny's accomplishments in Korea as director of foreign affairs and vice-minister of the Home Office between 1886 and 1890 are more controversial. Swartout credits him with at least partial success for his part in concluding the Franco-Korean Treaty of 1886 and the Russo-Korean Trade Agreement of 1888, the British evacuation of Kŏmundo, and in Kojong's establishment of a permanent legation in the United States.[71] Lew, however, portrays Denny as a failure, because his goal for the modernization and independence of Korea was not realized and because he had no compelling vision and blueprint for modernizing Korea.[72] As a later American adviser pointed out, in connection with von Möllendorff, one of the many problems of the Koreans in modernizing their country in those years was that there were too few advisers for jobs that were too big.[73]

In 1890 General Charles W. LeGendre succeeded Denny. LeGendre, a military adventurer of French extraction but a naturalized American, had been an adviser to the Japanese Foreign Office between 1872 and 1875, and had inspired the Japanese to become an expansionist power.[74] Korean Minister Kim Ka-jin in Tokyo, an enemy of Yüan, was mainly responsible for recruiting LeGendre.[75] Kojong was pleased with him, in the hope that he might be able to put China at a further distance from Korea. American Minister Heard, in Seoul, was also happy with him, as he felt that LeGendre would be more successful than his predecessor. Despite these expectations, LeGendre, as a diplomatic adviser and reformer, gave a poor performance, partly because of Yüan's opposition and partly because of his own inability.[76]

Another American adviser in Korea, Clarence R. Greathouse, was a lawyer and the former consul general in Yokohama.[77] A vice-minister of the Home Office and associate director of the telegraph and postal service, he performed his duties more credibly than LeGendre. But his achievements in Korea can hardly be compared with those of Gustave E. Boissonade in Japan.[78]

William Sands, another American adviser to Emperor Kojong, did his best to balance Russia and Japan against each other in the interest of Korea, but without success.[79] Sands, at best, held mixed feelings toward Korea. He considered Kojong to be politically confused and weak in personality, and felt no affection toward the Koreans.[80]

The last American adviser to the Korean government, Durham White Stevens, was in fact a secret Japanese agent, paid and instructed by the Japanese government between 1904 and 1907.[81] He served as "hands and feet" of the Japanese Foreign Office in the final stage of the demise of Korean independence. Like President Roosevelt, Stevens believed that Japan deserved Korea, just as the United States deserved the Philippines. Kojong and his countrymen, however, welcomed Stevens in the belief that they could count on him because he was an American; but they were soon double-crossed. In the spring of 1908 he went to the United States, not for the Korean cause but to justify Japanese control of Korea. Stevens died on March 25, 1908, victim of a Korean assassin's bullet; and two years later, Korea was annexed by the Japanese.[82]

In education, George W. Gilmore, Homer B. Hulbert, and Delzell A. Bunker signed two-year contracts with the Korean government and arrived in Seoul in July 1886. Unlike the earlier military advisers, these American teachers were highly qualified and dedicated instructors; and despite their low salaries they had a strong desire to found a university. Among other subjects, they taught English, social sciences, and natural sciences at the royal school. Within a few years, nonetheless, all three left the school because of inadequate salaries and the lack of government support for the school. In 1894, disappointed with the failure of the royal school the king turned to British teachers to start another government school, as he had done with the military training school.

American response to Korea's request for agricultural experts and technicians was also half-hearted. The U.S. Department of Agriculture provided a Korean model farm (called "American Farm") with a variety of seeds, agricultural tools, and California cattle, but not with agricultural personnel.

Official American Representatives in Korea

Although the accomplishments of the American military and political advisers in Korea were disappointing to the Koreans (except for a few, like Dye and Denny), the performances of the American diplomats in Korea seemed considerably encouraging. Trying to implement the instructions from the Department of State, however, these diplomats had run into several difficulties. First, they had to fight China's unwarranted interference in the affairs of Korea before 1895. Second, they had to cope with Japan's growing domination of Korea, especially after 1895. Third, they were repeatedly reminded by their superiors in Washington that they must maintain strict neutrality in all international and domestic struggles. Fourth, they could hardly count on Kojong, as he was too often and too easily intimidated by the Chinese, or the Russians, or the Japanese. Despite such difficulties, however, these American officials—with a few exceptions—left worthwhile records and impacts on Korea.

Lucius H. Foote, the first American envoy extraordinary and minister plenipotentiary, also left positive legacies in Korea. He strongly supported the independence of Korea vis-à-vis China and upheld Kojong's idea of hiring American advisers. It was Foote who suggested that the king send the first Korean mission to the United States in 1883, not only to show the world that Korea, after all, had become sovereign and independent but also to win, for all Koreans, the benefits of American civilization. His strong support of Korea's hiring of American advisers was a sound, practical, and feasible policy; yet his representation of the United States as a benevolent and moral power to King Kojong—unless he himself believed such a naive and half-truthful perception—was misguided. In view of the realities of international power politics, it would have been better if Foote had given Kojong the kind of advice that German Chancellor Otto von Bismarck had given the Iwakura Mission of Japan in 1871. Nevertheless, his attempt to bring American business interests into Korea was a valid and beneficial policy for both Korea and the United States. Finally, disappointed with the reduction of his rank to minister resident and consul general, Foote abruptly left Korea in 1885 and was succeeded by a young naval officer, George C. Foulk.

Foulk, a strong advocate of independence and modernization for Korea, became, as one historian expressed it, "a figure almost without blemish in Korean historiography."[83] Korean historians of South Korean orientation universally praise Foulk's effort,[84] although American historians hotly debate the merits of his performance.[85] If Foulk had served in China and involved himself in modernizing China, as he did in Korea, then Foulk would undoubtedly occupy a negative place in Chinese historiography. Unlike the Korean leadership (Kojong), which welcomed Western advisers and diplomats who supported the modernization of Korea, the Chinese leadership (Tz'u-hsi) rejected or distrusted Westerners advocating the modernization of China.[86]

Unfortunately for Korean progress and independence, as well as for the diplomatic career of Foulk, he was declared *persona non grata* by Korean Foreign Minister Kim Yun-sik, a Chinese puppet. Kim told Foulk to leave Korea, because of pressure and manipulation by Chinese Resident Yüan Shih-k'ai in Seoul, who considered Foulk's pro-Korean attitude detrimental to the Chinese interest in Korea. King Kojong and American Minister Hugh Dinsmore were unable to prevent Foulk from leaving Korea in 1887, symbolizing the dilemma that Kojong faced in modernizing his kingdom in the face of Chinese opposition.

In June 1886, Minister Resident William H. Parker arrived at the American legation in Seoul and Kojong told him that he looked upon the United States as his best friend; he then asked Parker to request President Cleveland to permit Foulk to enter the Korean civil service. Unfortunately, Parker, the first superintendent of the Confederate Naval Academy and former president of Maryland Agricultural College, proved to be a sorry and hopeless dipsomaniac, and stayed in Korea for only three months.

Although the name of W. W. Rockhill is prominent in connection with Hay's Open Door Policy, his brief service in Korea as American chargé d'affaires, between December 11, 1886, and April 3, 1887, is not notable, except for what he did to avoid a constitutional scruple by making resigned or noncommissioned American officers come to Korea. However, he had great influence on Hay, Root, and Roosevelt in formulating the pro-Japanese American policy before and during the Russo-Japanese War.[87]

Between 1887 and 1890, Minister Dinsmore continued the pro-Korean, pro-reform, and anti-Chinese posture and policy initiated by Foote and Foulk. He fought many battles against Yüan for the cause of Korean independence and supported Kojong's establishment of a permanent legation in the United States in 1887 and 1888. Kojong's confidence in Dinsmore was so strong that he asked Bayard to permit Dinsmore to resign from the American diplomatic service and accept the position of an adviser to the Korean government, as a successor to Judge Denny. But Bayard refused, because it would have made the job of Dinsmore's successor "difficult" and might have complicated Sino-Korean-American relations because of China's claim to suzerainty over Korea.

During his tenure in Korea, between 1890 and 1893, Minister Resident Augustine Heard also sympathized with Kojong, as he suffered China's domination and Japan's growing and aggressive influence in Korea. In general, Heard kept a very low posture in performing his duties, and is said to have been dominated by his legation secretary, Allen.

Minister Resident Sill's accomplishment in Korea between 1894 and 1897 remains a subject of debate.[88] Among other things, he played an outstanding role in enunciating a kind of open-door policy in Korea against the Japanese aggression. As were Foulk and Dinsmore, he was repeatedly warned by his superiors in Washington not to be concerned with Korean affairs, except when America's legitimate interests were involved. In 1897 he was recalled by the McKinley administration, largely because of his troubles with the Japanese in Korea.

Sill was replaced by his subordinate, Dr. Horace N. Allen, a strong-willed and famous missionary-diplomat. Allen's position on the independence and interests of Korea seems complex, if not ambivalent or devious. He did believe in the economic and industrial development of Korea through American investment. On the subject of Korean independence, however, he fought against Chinese dominance in the peninsula, believing that Japan should have the paramount influence. When the Russians tried to control Korea, he supported the Japanese; when the Japanese attempted to swallow Korea, he struggled against them. But it proved vain in the end. During all this he was somehow able to lead Kojong, and many of his advisers, to believe that the United States was the only power acting disinterestedly toward Korea.

In March 1905, Allen was abruptly replaced by Minister Resident Edwin V. Morgan, a friend of President Roosevelt, in order to make the anticipated American diplomatic exit from Korea smoother and easier, in December of the same year. Thus the United States, the first Western treaty power and first Western nation that established a legation in Seoul, became the first power to withdraw its legation from Korea—"like the stampede of rats from a sinking ship," in the words of the American legation secretary, Willard Straight.[89] Allen lamented that "we might have given them [the Koreans] an expression of sympathy and waited until the funeral was over before nailing up the coffin."[90]

American Missionary and Business Interests in Korea

It is true that, in view of his Confucianism and of the unfortunate war between Korea and France in the 1860s (on account of his father's persecution of French missionaries), Kojong was opposed to the Christian missionary movement in his kingdom. Even so, in dealing with American missionary efforts in Korea he proved to be very flexible and pragmatic. When Dr. Horace Allen, the first American medical missionary, was sent to Korea from China by the American Presbyterian Board of Missions, Kojong asked Minister Foote if he were a missionary. When Foote replied that Allen was a "physician" to the American legation, Kojong seemed satisfied. Eventually, Allen became the most active American in Korea. As a court physician, an American legation secretary, and later as an American minister in Seoul, Allen played a crucial role not only in educational, medical, and missionary movements but also in diplomatic and political affairs in Korea.

Allen was soon followed by many other American missionaries, whom he introduced to the Korean court. Dr. William Scranton, a Methodist, and Dr. John Heron, a Presbyterian, were appointed to Allen's royal hospital. A Presbyterian nurse, Annie Ellers, became a physician to Queen Min. Allen also helped a Presbyterian, Horace G. Underwood, and a Methodist, Henry G. Appenzeller, to obtain quasi-governmental status in educational works.

After realizing that the efforts of American missionaries could contribute to the development and progress of his country in medical, educational, social, and other areas, Kojong not only tolerated but encouraged their secular works.[91] Thus American diplomatic and missionary works became almost inseparable, although some American diplomats (such as Foulk) tried to separate missionary from political and diplomatic activities.[92] In time, many American missionaries played prominent roles in various aspects of Korean life.[93] Nevertheless, missionaries were not particularly successful in converting the natives, for in 1905 there were only about 40,000 Korean Christians— a little over 1 percent of the converts the American missionaries had made in the world.[94] Also, the majority of American missionaries in Korea, though opposed to Chinese domination, generally supported Japanese control of the country.[95]

One of the most important reasons for America's "opening" of Korea was investment and trade. Kojong felt that the so-called American benevolence, morality, and Christianity— strong though they might be—might not be a sufficient ground for an American guarantee of the integrity and independence of his kingdom. As an incentive to do good things for Korea, he believed the United States must have strong economic stakes in his country. Therefore, as a means of inducing and strengthening American interests in Korea, Kojong encouraged American investment and trade. He further reasoned that enhanced American business interests in Korea would mean not only political commitment but also a boost to Korean development and modernization. To be sure, American investment became significant, at least from the standpoint of Korea, as Americans were put in charge of building railroads, streetcars, a public telegram system, and the Unsan gold mining.[96]

Nevertheless, American trade in Korea was quite disappointing. For example, the annual average of American trade with Korea between 1894 and 1904 was about $200,000, ranging between $100 and $1,000,000. It was less than one-hundredth of 1 percent of America's foreign trade.[97] Thus the American economic interest in Korea in 1904 and 1905 was almost negligible.

Conclusion

During the twenty-three years of official diplomatic intercourse with the United States, Korean foreign policy was in the hands of one monarch, who ruled continuously throughout the era. American foreign policy, on the other hand, was conducted by five presidents and ten secretaries of state, with nine different officers charged with the affairs of the American legation in Seoul. Interestingly enough, what Kojong wanted from all of them was various kinds of help in modernizing and developing his kingdom. In addition, he wished the United States—a faraway and benevolent Christian country (in his perception)—to become a kind of new elder brother and guarantee the independence of Korea, chiefly through offering its "good offices," but also through other means in time of international crisis. In a way, Kojong and his reform-minded advisers wanted the United States to do for their country what China had done in the past.

To induce and strengthen American interests in Korea, he encouraged American economic activities in the peninsula.

Even in regard to missionary movements, the good Confucian monarch not only tolerated but supported their secular works, since they were contributing to his program of modernization. Kojong felt that his expectations of the U.S. government were fully justified, in view of the friendly and amicable attitudes and behavior of American representatives at their legation in Seoul. Unfortunately for him and his kingdom, even after Washington had largely failed to meet the high expectations that he and some of the American diplomats in Seoul had placed in the United States, Kojong either failed or refused to see the uselessness of his faith in America.

So far as the U.S. government was concerned, to justify an active interest in Korea so as to guarantee its independence, there should have been at least a few important points of mutuality between the two countries. The integrity and independence of Korea should have been vital to the security of the United States, politically or militarily or economically. However, before 1905—unlike the situation since 1945 (as expounded by Robert Oliver in chapter 5 and by Tae-Hwan Kwak and Wayne Patterson in chapter 6)—none of these bonds existed between the two countries. Moreover (as Harrington explains so lucidly in chapter 3), American presidents were preoccupied mainly with domestic issues, for reasons of economic improvement and the next election. Consequently, the American government refused to break the well-established, traditional policy, more than a century old, of noninvolvement in the affairs of Asian countries through entanglement in the complex political problems of a faraway peninsula kingdom.

To be sure, America supported the independence of Korea and sympathized with Kojong's effort to modernize his kingdom; but beyond this the government—whether under a Republican or a Democratic administration—did not intend to go. Thus in the struggle with China over suzerainty and dependency, the United States maintained "pro-Korean neutrality," without taking meaningful action. Moreover, at the repeated Korean request for "good offices" on the eve of the Sino-Japanese War, Gresham, while urging the Japanese government to avoid "an unjust war" in Korea, on the same day assured the Japanese minister in Washington of America's neutrality and strongly rejected any kind of unilateral, bilateral, or multilateral intervention in favor of Korea. Also, by the time of the Russo-Japanese War of 1904 and 1905, the United States had shifted its orientation toward Korea: from benevolent but strictly neutral to strongly pro-Japanese and anti-Korean, thereby supporting and encouraging the Japanese takeover of Korea.

The wisdom and far-sightedness of Roosevelt's pro-Japanese policy has been hotly debated in view of America's eventual opposition to Japanese expansionism in Asia, as evidenced in the Root-Takahira Notes of 1908, the Lansing-Ishii Agreement of 1917, the Stimson Doctrine of 1931, and, finally, the Japanese attack on Pearl Harbor in 1941. Nonetheless, as viewed in terms of the international realities of 1904 and 1905, and in light of her negligible strategic, political, and economic interests in Korea, the American policy of realism in dealing with Korea and Japan can hardly be criticized or condemned.

On the other hand, there seems to be much room for criticism of the bungling way the United States handled the selection and dispatch of its military and other advisers to Korea. Since the United States opened the Korean door to the West, since it wanted to see Korea become a stable and independent kingdom, and since it assumed an important role in Eastern affairs (e.g., the modernization of Japan), it could have employed a much more competent and efficient method of selecting (and sending) advisers to Korea, without violating the spirit and letter of America's neutral policy in the area. Before 1895, after all, even the governments of China and Japan (though not Resident Yüan) wanted the Korean government to hire American advisers. Although the United States long held to a policy of sympathy and neutrality in Korean affairs, it finally adopted a policy of "giving up" on Korea.

In view of the fact that both the Sino-Japanese War of 1894 and 1895 and the Russo-Japanese War of 1904 and 1905 had broken out mainly, or at least partly, owing to the weakness of the Korean government in military, political, and other areas, the hostilities would most likely have been avoided if China had let Korea alone in her attempt at modernization during the 1880s and early 1890s, if the United States had given more vigorous support to the modernization of Korea, and if Japan had exemplified more patience and justice in dealing with Korea in the 1890s and 1900s.

Whether Japanese policy toward Korea between 1894 and 1905 was cooperative or imperialistic is still vigorously debated among East Asian and American diplomatic historians. Some insist that the Japanese policy toward Korea during this period was "cautious" and "cooperative."[98] Others argue that Japanese policy toward the peninsula was "aggressive," "careless," and even imperialistic.[99]

Even if the American government had given positive support to Korea by selecting and sending a number of competent advisers, Kojong would still have had a great deal of difficulty in modernizing his country for a variety of reasons, including: lack of progressive Korean leadership, paucity of necessary funds, excessive strife of factionalism and corruption within the country, Chinese opposition (before 1894), Japanese bullying tactics and behavior (after 1894), and finally his own inconsistent policies in the 1890s and 1900s.[100] However, without a sufficient number of effective advisers, it would have been very difficult for him to modernize his country, even if he did not have the aforementioned problems. Thus one could say that one of the most important reasons for Kojong's failure in reforming his kingdom was the absence of sufficient numbers of competent American advisers who could have served Korea with some long-range goals and blueprints, and could have become not only sources of inspiration but actual contributions to the development of Korea. No wonder some historians characterize Korean-American relations to 1910 as a "one-sided affair" or a "one-sided love."[101] Certainly Kojong's unwarranted faith in the United States, in the world of power politics, confirms that description.

That fact leads to a pertinent question with regard to Kojong's statesmanship and character: How should historians view him as a ruler and reformer during such a critical period? Although his character and statesmanship is one of the most controversial subjects in the late Yi Dynasty, some historians insist that Kojong was a flexible, pragmatic, bold, and innovative reformer, at least in the late 1870s and 1880s.[102] Others describe him as a weak, confused, secretive, and intrigue-minded ruler.[103] Realistically, the negative description seems more valid for the period after 1895, when he experienced the assassination of his wife at the hands (indirectly) of Japanese Minister Miura and constant intimidation by the Japanese. Earlier, between the late 1870s and early 1890s, he was indeed a pragmatic, flexible, and innovative reformer—probably not as much as his counterpart in Japan, Emperor Meiji,[104] but more than Empress Dowager Tz'u-hsi of China. The pragmatism and flexibility of Kojong and his reform-minded advisers can be attributed, in part, to the fact that Korea (unlike China, and to a lesser extent like Japan) had a tradition of borrowing from abroad.

Largely because of Korea's historical experiences with her neighbors, Kojong and his advisers did not think of making their country strong and independent on their own. Kojong felt that his country could become stable, modern, and independent under the protection of, or in alliance with, great powers, such as China, Russia, Japan, or the United States. Since China had been rapidly declining, she was out of the question. Kojong's first choice was the United States, for the reasons explained in this chapter; but American aid came too slowly. So in 1884 he quietly took the side of pro-Japanese progressives, until the Chinese quelled them. In 1885, he tacitly agreed with von Möllendorff in bringing Russia into Korea; but the ploy was crushed by the Chinese, Japanese, and British, and even by the Americans. Besides, Russia at that time was not ready to move into Korea. After the Japanese moved into Korea on a larger scale in 1894 and 1895, Kojong felt they were overaggressive and overambitious; so he clung to his faith in the United States, though it all proved in vain in the end.

As it turned out, the empire of Japan became strong and modernized whereas the kingdom of Korea became absorbed by Japan. Thus Emperor Meiji became a winner while Emperor Kojong became a loser—the point being that it is very easy to praise a winner and criticize a loser. One wonders what would have happened if Kojong had been the emperor of Japan and Meiji the ruler of Korea, or if Korea were located where Japan is and Japan where Korea is.

3

An American View of Korean-American Relations, 1882–1905

Fred Harvey Harrington

When I wrote my book on Korean-American relations, more than forty years ago, there was little interest in Korea in the United States. So little, in fact, that my publisher and I decided to leave *Korea* out of the main title.[1] Since then, post–World War II involvement in now-divided Korea has increased America's interest; and scholars, using Asian as well as Western sources, have produced high-quality monographs on the domestic and foreign problems of the Yi Dynasty (1392–1910) during its final decades.[2]

Even so, we still lack full understanding of why the United States behaved as it did in the half-century between the American Civil War and the Japanese takeover of Korea (1865–1905/10). For a time in the 1870s and 1880s the American government appeared to be aggressively interested in Korea, in the imperialist fashion of nineteenth-century European powers. The United States shed a good deal of Korean blood in 1871, and a dozen years later was first among Western nations to establish a legation in the Korean capital.

Then the situation changed. From the middle 1880s on, those in charge in Washington showed themselves to be indifferent; and in 1905 President Theodore Roosevelt endorsed the Japanese seizure of Korea and abruptly withdrew the American legation from Seoul. Yet in those twenty years of unconcern in Washington, Americans in Korea consistently—and tragically—led King (later Emperor) Kojong to believe he could count on United States assistance in his efforts to maintain his country's independence, as Professor Lee's essay has demonstrated.

Clues to this peculiar mixture of positions can be found in Western attitudes toward "backward" regions, in domestic conditions inside the United States, and in the tendency of Americans overseas to go beyond the instructions from Washington.

Aggressive Action

In the late nineteenth century, Western powers made vigorous efforts to secure economic, strategic, and cultural control of much of Asia and the Pacific, Africa, and Latin America. Usually this meant annexing colonies or establishing other kinds of dependency relationships, alone or in combination with competing powers. Inhabitants of affected areas were seldom consulted, for the dominant imperialist theories labeled these peoples inferior and unenlightened—in contrast with the West. Given this conviction of superiority, the powers rarely hesitated to use force when the "natives" objected to their advance.[3] Indeed, it was thought to be the "duty" of "civilized" nations to impose their will on, and carry the "benefits" of Western culture to, remote regions.[4]

The United States did not entirely accept European models for imperialism. Most European powers were aristocratic monarchies whereas Americans claimed to be interested in exporting democratic republican values to the less-developed lands. And, except for parts of Latin America and the Pacific Ocean, the United States was less interested in control or exclusive rights than in getting equal opportunity—an "open door"—for trade, investment, and missionary endeavor.

But like the Europeans, Americans were intensely nationalistic, the Civil War having added to an already strong conviction of their superiority. Also like Europeans, they felt certain that people who were not white and Christian were inferior, and need not be consulted or treated as equals. Instead, such people could be pushed a little— "punished," if need be—as Americans introduced trading goods, the Bible, and the ballot box. "Always for the benefit of the Asiatics themselves," said one expansionist, since Christianity and civilization "will bestow inestimable benefits upon distant semi-barbarians and alien races."[5]

Americans had always been trade minded. From the beginning, presidents and congressmen had promoted exports and the carrying trade. Exports exceeded imports for the first time in the 1870s, as they would for a century thereafter. Besides, trade was changing character. Long an agricultural nation, sending farm products to Europe, the United States was adding industrial strength and would soon pass the European powers in coal, iron, and steel production.[6] That suggested the need for new markets and new sources of raw materials, which brought to mind Latin America and the Far East. Panics and depression, from 1873 to the 1890s, would underscore the fact that productive capacity exceeded domestic consumption, further indicating the need to push for foreign markets.[7] Robert W. Shufeldt, soon to be prominent in Korean matters, said this bluntly in 1878: "At least one-third of our mechanical and agricultural products are in excess of our own wants, and we *must* export these products."[8]

American economic activity in Asia and the Pacific was small, compared to United States trade with Europe and Latin America. Still, the Eastern trade was important, and many thought that it would be more so.[9] American whalers, explorers, and China traders were active early in the nineteenth century. Then, with the acquisition of California and Oregon in the 1840s, the United States became a Pacific power. Early in the next decade, Commodore Matthew C. Perry used the threat of force to open Japan to foreign commerce.

American merchants and missionaries had already located in China and Hawaii; soon they would be in evidence from Siberia to Samoa, Fiji, Borneo, and western Australia. Although their numbers were few and some of the traders were reckless adventurers, such individuals on occasion became the advance agents of empire. Certainly they worried such expanding powers as Great Britain and, later, Germany. "Of course America is a go-ahead country and will push in wherever she can," complained one Britisher, adding that the Americans "probably . . . hope to be masters of the Pacific presently."[10] (And some did; Shufeldt was only one of many who predicted that "the Pacific Ocean is to become at no distant day the commercial domain of America.")[11]

Korean-American relations began in 1866 because of the activities of one of those go-ahead trader-adventurers: an American, W. B. Preston.[12] The story has all the ingredients of the imperialist age: insistence on trade, missionary zeal, willingness to use force. The *General Sherman*, a heavily armed and aptly named American merchant vessel, tried to force the reluctant Koreans to abandon isolation and allow trade with the outside world. It was the worst possible timing, for the powerful Taewŏn'gun (young King Kojong's father) was determined to uphold the Hermit Kingdom's antitrade and antimissionary traditions.[13] In so doing, he had just executed several French Catholic priests and many Korean converts.[14]

Though warned, the *General Sherman* pushed into forbidden waters and fired its guns as it proceeded upriver toward P'yŏngyang, now North Korea's capital. Owner Preston and his American captain seized a local official; and they allowed their interpreter, a British Protestant missionary, to go ashore, preach, distribute Bible texts, and mix with proscribed Korean

Catholic converts.[15] Incautious in every way, the invaders then ran aground.

As the Korean reports stated, the local people were outraged at the "crafty and beast-like foreigners." ("The barbarians from beyond the seas have violated our borders and invaded our land.") Whereupon they destroyed the *General Sherman,* killing all hands, including three Americans. ("The wretched foreigners were . . . hacked to pieces by the furious mob.")[16]

Obviously, those who organized and handled this expedition were wholly at fault.[17] But the *General Sherman* was an American vessel, and American lives had been lost. "Pirates of the worst kind . . . capture a ship, pillage it, burn it, and kill all the crew," cried the *New York Commercial Advertiser.*[18] "Until the Government takes efficient action on this case," added Admiral H. H. Bell, "our countrymen who lawfully navigate the seas adjacent to Korea will be in peril."[19]

Taking up the matter, the U.S. government considered "reprisals" and decided to use the incident to press Korea to permit foreign trade.[20] The *General Sherman* was still much in mind when the Washington authorities directed the American minister to China, F. F. Low, and Admiral John Rodgers to try their luck in Korea (1871). ("The errand of the *General Sherman* was probably illegal," said Rodgers, "but that does not absolve the Government from obligation to inquire into the reason for putting them to death.")[21]

Instructed to "avoid a conflict by force unless it cannot be avoided without dishonor," those in charge of the Low-Rodgers expedition soon decided that honor required combat.[22] Trouble began when American vessels on survey assignment approached Korea's barriers of defense near Chemulp'o (Inch'ŏn), the gateway to Seoul. This drew fire, which was returned. Since the Americans had the better of this exchange, things might have been left at that. Low and Rodgers, however, had the typical reaction of nineteenth-century Westerners dealing with people they considered "semi-barbarous." There had been an insult to the Stars and Stripes and the Koreans had "set at defiance the law of nations as well as the laws of humanity." Besides, the Koreans refused to apologize for this "wanton and unprovoked attack" or for the *General Sherman* affair.[23] Their officials had used "insulting and abusive language,"[24] and they had not agreed to open trade. So they must be "punished."[25]

Then came what the *New York Herald*, with typical condescension toward Asians, called "Our Little War with the Heathen."[26] The landing party moved into action with enthusiasm. Many of the officers and men had been too young for Civil War action "and wanted a taste of fire"; they were "spoiling for a brush."[27] Destroying the forts on Kanghwa Island, the Americans slaughtered at least 250 brave but ill-armed Koreans, with the loss of only three American lives.[28] (The enemy "fought with desperate courage" but "many were shot like rabbits.")

This was the largest body count of Asians killed by Americans until the Filipino "insurrection" of 1899.[29] It was the largest number of Koreans killed by any foreign power in those last years before the Hermit Kingdom was dragged reluctantly into world diplomacy. And this should be remembered by Americans with a sense of shame. Yet protests were few. Since the Americans had departed after the bloodletting, the Korean conclusion was that the invaders had been defeated.[30] Certainly they had not gained their objective of a trade treaty.[31]

Nor was there much criticism back home when reports of the action reached the United States. Indeed, there was less condemnation than forty years before, when Commodore John Downes killed 100 Sumatrans for a minor interference with the American pepper trade.[32] "Outrages on our sailors have been avenged" was the front-page judgment of the *New York Times*, under the headline "Speedy and Effective Punishment of the Barbarians." It had been "Splendid Artillery Practice," added the *Tribune*.[33]

The American government never apologized for letting so much Korean blood. And when it came to trying again for a trade treaty (1878–82), the United States assigned the negotiating responsibility not to a civilian, but to a navy man, Robert W. Shufeldt. This officer believed, and stated flatly, that to an Oriental "the only appeal or argument appreciated is *force*,"[34] that in gunpowder one found "the power as well as the justice of civilization."[35] In other words, if gentle persuasion failed, a "civilized" power like the United States would be justified in using the threat of force, or force itself, to end Korean isolation.

As it turned out, force was not needed; Shufeldt did not even have to negotiate with the Koreans. Instead, it was possible to work out a Korean-American trade–and–good offices treaty in China with Viceroy Li Hung-chang (1882). The Chinese still claimed suzerain rights in Korea, which enabled Li to press the Koreans to agree to diplomatic and trade relations with the United States and the western European powers. Deeply concerned about Japanese and Russian ambitions in Northeast Asia, the viceroy saw Korean treaties with others as one way of checking Japan and Russia.[36]

As Li judged the situation, there were good reasons for starting with the United States. Though haughty toward non-Western people and wretched in their treatment of Chinese immigrants, Americans seemed not to be interested in grabbing large chunks of territory on the Asian mainland. ("The United States . . . has never had any territorial ambitions," Li told the Koreans.)[37] Besides, the American republic, with its antiquated fleet, still counted as a minor power; it was not a major threat in the Far East.

Koreans who remembered the bloody record of 1871 had their doubts about Li's strategy. "America is the enemy of Korea, and once threatened to bombard our cities," a Korean official told the Japanese in 1880; "we will never accept any proposition made to us for friendly intercourse with America."[38] Hun-

dreds of Confucianist conservatives, in mourning clothes, held
vigil outside the royal palace in an effort to persuade the king
not to abandon Korea's traditional isolation.[39]

In time, however, the Koreans in the government decided to
go along with Li's treaty. They valued China's advice; and King
Kojong knew he would need help against possible aggressors.
So there were formalities at Chemulp'o, near the 1871 bat-
tleground;[40] and in 1883 the United States established its legation in Seoul.

The American republic considered stronger moves even after
China brought in the United States as a sort of protector of
Korea. On more than one occasion American diplomats and
naval officers recommended taking over Port Hamilton, or
some other Korean site, for a coaling station and naval base. It
was assumed that there would be negotiations before or after
the occupation; but those who proposed the action had no
objection to outright seizure if it proved necessary or conven-
ient. This was the case even with diplomats who were rated
"friends of Korea." Eventually, the navy's general board dropped
the Korean-base idea—for strategic reasons, however, not out
of consideration for Korea.[41] The Koreans were not consulted
on the matter.

The same tendency to ignore the wishes of Koreans and their
government was evident on the religious side. The Shufeldt
treaty did not authorize Christian proselytizing, which was forbidden under Korean law. It was generally known, as one missionary admitted in 1892, that every American diplomat who
went to Seoul "construed the treaty . . . to mean that . . . teaching and preaching Christianity is not allowed."[42] But Protestant
missionaries came from the United States and soon were dis-
tributing material, preaching, and seeking converts, in defiance
of legal prohibitions.[43] Mindful of the church vote and convinced of the value of spreading the Word, the United States
government provided support. The first American missionary to

reside in Korea was "protected" by being made legation physician; and Washington officials sometimes appeared to be more
pro-missionary than their agents in the field.[44]

In time the Korean court concluded that missionaries from
the United States were not very dangerous and that they made
medical and educational contributions. Still, their presence was
disturbing in troubled times, as during the "Baby War" of 1888,
when Christians were accused of boiling babies for food and
cutting off the breasts of Korean women to get condensed
milk.[45] There were no tragedies to compare with the slaughter
of Catholics in 1866; but in its religious policies the American
government showed again how little respect it had for the laws
and customs of "backward" nations.

Retreat to an Inactive Policy

After shedding Korean blood, after leading the Western world
in breaking down Korean isolation, after looking with favor on
a challenge to Korea's religious policies—after all that, the policymakers in Washington pulled back. Instead of continuing an
aggressive role in Korea, they retreated to a passive, inactive
position. They maintained this posture from the middle 1880s
to 1905, when they led the West in leaving Korea, as they had led
in moving to Korea two decades earlier.[46]

The process began almost immediately after ratification of
the Shufeldt treaty. Just a few months after the State Department had sent its first envoy extraordinary and minister plenipotentiary to the Korean capital, Congress reduced the rank of
the American representative to minister resident—without objection from the White House.[47] Thereafter the United States
often left the Seoul post unfilled, or in charge of officials too
low in rank to command the attention of the State Department.
Dispatches from Korea went unanswered for long periods or

were not answered at all. One important message, as Secretary of State Frederick T. Frelinghuysen admitted, was "mislaid."[48]

This forgotten message contained a request for American advisers, and nothing was more important to King Kojong, who needed experts to help him strengthen his country and make Korean independence a reality. China, Russia, and Japan were willing to supply advisers; but with their expertise came threats of outside control.[49] Thus the State Department's failure to act on this and later requests was damaging to Korea.

When the State Department finally took up the topic, it instructed its representatives in Korea not to press for American advisers ("it is not deemed expedient").[50] And when Americans *did* take up such assignments, they were told that "the United States will not, under any circumstances, be drawn into any complications which may arise out of your troubles. You do not represent the Department of State or American influence in any way. You are an adventurer as far as we are concerned." William Franklin Sands, the adviser to whom Secretary of State John Hay addressed these words, felt that this attitude "killed any hope of pulling the Koreans out of their troubles. What they wanted was not an individual American, but the good will of the American government."[51]

There were other consequences. When the United States opted out of providing advisers on an official basis, Kojong acquired Americans through other channels—as sorry a batch of "experts" as one could assemble. Some were incompetent and/or corrupt. Many were intemperate, quarrelsome, and bitterly anti-Korean.[52] Others—accepted by the court because they were Americans—served Chinese or Japanese interests rather than those of the United States or Korea.[53]

The dominant note in Washington was indifference rather than hostility. None of the five occupants of the White House from 1882 to 1905, and none of their ten secretaries of state, gave more than passing notice to relations with Korea. This left

action, or the lack of it, to lower-level State Department officers. Most of these knew little and cared less about Korea, and
were disinclined to work on topics that did not interest their
superiors.[54]

The most enduring of these lesser officials was Alvey A. Adee,
the assistant secretary of state and well-known careerist. Although Adee was Europe-minded, and took a dim view of most
Orientals and many of the Americans who represented the
United States in Asia, he was often called upon to handle the
Korean correspondence or to scribble drafts for those above
him. His approach was to play down Korea, to oppose any move
toward a more active policy.[55]

Also in the picture, after 1893, was William Woodville Rockhill, the China expert on whom Secretary Hay and President
Theodore Roosevelt depended for advice on the Far East. (He
was, said Roosevelt, the "author of and sponsor for our Asiatic
policy.")[56] Unlike his State Department colleagues, Rockhill
knew a good deal about Korea. He had served as chargé d'affaires in Seoul for a few months in 1886–87, after which he had
written a learned paper on Sino-Korean relations. This paper,
which could be called an endorsement of the Korean drive for
independence, explained the limitations on China's suzerainty
claims.[57]

Neither residence nor research, however, led Rockhill to rec-
ommend increased American activity in Korea. He found little
to praise in Korean customs.[58] He considered Kojong's court in
"utter ignorance" of how to handle ordinary business, let alone
contend with greedy foreign powers.[59] Therefore, Rockhill concluded, the United States should stay out of the line of fire,
should ignore Korean pleas for help against her foes. This was
his advice to policymakers, and helps explain why he favored
the Japanese seizure of Korea in 1905.

Important though he was (critically important, perhaps, in
1905), Rockhill did not create his government's low-profile

Korean policy. That policy was in place before Rockhill joined
the State Department's headquarters staff in 1893, even before
his tour of duty in Seoul. Mistaken or not, the policy was clear
and consistent. The United States government gave assistance—passive assistance, most of the time—to American
businessmen and missionary societies interested in Korea. It
insisted on treating Korea as an independent sovereign nation,
even when outside powers were controlling, or trying to control, Kojong's court.[60] And since the Shufeldt treaty mentioned
"good offices," the State Department was willing to offer
(though not press) them in times of crisis.[61] But that was all.
Time after time, Washington refused to take steps to support
Korean independence or to check aggressors who threatened
Korea's freedom of action.

Instructions to American representatives in Seoul were blunt
and to the point:[62]

> Seoul is the center of . . . intrigues. . . . It is clearly the interest
> of the United States to hold aloof from all this and do nothing
> nor be drawn into anything which would look like taking sides
> with any of the contestants or entering the lists of intrigue for
> our own benefit. Hence the exercise of the utmost discretion on
> your part is necessary [Democratic Secretary of State Thomas F.
> Bayard to George C. Foulk, August 19, 1885].

> I cannot too urgently caution you against any remarks or sug-
> gestions which might have the appearance of advice regarding
> the military defenses or operations of Korea [Republican Secre-
> tary of State James G. Blaine to Legation Secretary Charles
> Chaillé-Long, March 15, 1889].

> The Department sees with disfavor your disposition to forget
> that you are not to interfere with local concerns and politics of
> Korea. . . . Your course in continued intermeddling with Korean
> political affairs in violation of repeated instructions noted with
> astonishment and emphatic disapproval. Cable briefly any expla-
> nation you have to make also answer whether you intend to

comply with instructions [Democratic Secretary of State Richard Olney to Minister John M. B. Sill, December 2, 1895, and
January 11, 1896].

Department instructions positively forbid you to mix in internal
affairs of the country. Explicit compliance therewith requested.

It behooves the United States and their representatives, as absolutely neutral parties, to say, or do nothing that can in any way be
construed as taking sides with or against any of the interested
powers. Any such partiality would not only be in itself improper,
but might have the undesirable and unfortunate effect of leading
the Koreans themselves to regard the United States as their
natural and only ally for any and all such purposes as Korea's
rulers might adopt. This Government is in no sense the coun-
sellor of Korea as to its internal destinies, neither is it bound to
Korea by any protective alliance [Republican Secretary of State
John Sherman to Ministers Sill, May 8, and Horace N. Allen,
November 19, 1897].

As for other Americans residing in Korea, Secretary Olney
(on Rockhill's advice?) told Minister Sill that he should inform
them to "refrain from any expression of opinion or from giving
advice," especially during crises. Missionaries should "strictly
confine themselves to the missionary work"; the legation
should "discourage and stop, if possible, the habit . . . of irre-
sponsible persons advising and attempting to control, through
irregular channels, the Government of that country."[63]

Here was full retreat from any thought of an active American
policy for Korea. And the State Department made sure that its
position was known and understood by releasing the text of
some of its sharper stay-out statements.

This did not mean that the United States was pulling out of
international competition in the nonindustrialized world. Selec-
tive retreats were standard in the age of high imperialism. Expansionist powers pushed forward with vigor, only to fall back
when they felt overextended—or when they found themselves

in regions fiercely contested and judged the game not worth the risk. Often, too, powers made deals with each other for sharing control or defining zones of interest. The American government did this in Samoa in 1889, working out a condominium arrangement with Germany and Great Britain (which was revised a decade later, with Britain receiving concessions for bowing out of the picture). Theodore Roosevelt's Taft-Katsura Memorandum of 1905 was another Great Power agreement, with Roosevelt acknowledging Japanese control of Korea while Japan recognized American ownership of the Philippine Islands.[64]

State Department thinking about Korea fitted this pattern. From the start, it was apparent that the kingdom was of only minor importance to the United States in strategic, economic, or other terms. It was worth some attention, but not if there were danger signals; and there were many. Just before and just after establishment of the American legation there were bloody uprisings in Seoul, involving China and Japan. Then, with Russia active in the north, Britain occupied Port Hamilton. The Korean capital was revealed as "the most slippery spot,"[65] with "diplomacy in the raw . . . without gloves, perfume or phrases."[66] If America persisted, she would have trouble with a variety of local factions and at least three outside powers, each of which had a larger stake in Korea than the United States.

Meanwhile, problems at home turned the attention of many Americans away from foreign lands. With the Democrats and Republicans almost evenly balanced, control of the White House and State Department shifted from one party to the other every four years from 1880 to 1896. This meant that American presidents and secretaries of state, being practical politicians, had to devote most of their energies to domestic politics,[67] pointing to the next election. And apart from campaigning, urgent domestic matters were overshadowing diplomacy: major economic depressions, post–Civil War sectional strife, monetary problems, and farm and labor unrest so severe as to make conservatives fear that revolution was imminent.[68]

Some politicians and business leaders proposed a vigorous foreign policy as a way out of domestic difficulties; but even they had little interest in places as distant as Korea.[69] Others opposed adventures overseas because they wanted to concentrate on home markets, or felt that the United States as yet lacked the financial resources to compete worldwide. Or they feared racial and other consequences of increased activity in "backward" areas.[70] Aware of this anti-imperialist sentiment, shown in congressional votes and other ways, expansionists tended to concentrate on regions less remote than Asia, hence of more immediate interest to the American public: Hawaii, for example, and northern Latin America.

Thus there was no chance that the United States would help build Korean defenses or provide significant military, economic, or diplomatic support when Korea was in trouble. Nor did the American government give serious thought to mounting or participating in a "Switzerland of Asia" effort to secure an international neutralization agreement to guarantee Korea's independence.[71]

Raising Korean Hopes

Why, then, did Kojong or any of his subjects count on or hope for help and guidance from the United States?[72]

He and they certainly had such hopes and expectations. In talking about the United States, the Korean ruler liked to use the term "elder brother," which called to mind the guardian relationship of Chinese suzerain tradition.[73] "We have the promise of America," he and his officials told visitors; "she will be our friend whatever happens." There was no doubt, they added, that America and like-minded European powers "would make it difficult for any one nation to ruthlessly take away their independence."[74]

Koreans who made such statements were aware that the United States had earlier shown strong interest in their country. Might it not again, since the Shufeldt treaty had contained half-promises that the United States would be helpful? The good-offices section of the treaty could be interpreted in various ways; but to the Korean court it symbolized friendship, plus a moral commitment to provide aid in times of crisis.[75]

Even more important was the behavior of the American community in Seoul: diplomats, advisers, missionaries, traders, and concession hunters. Year after year these people assured the Koreans that they could count on the United States; help would be forthcoming in due time. Since it never came, these comments were misleading, and contributed to the sense of betrayal in Korea when the United States withdrew its legation in 1905.

In encouraging the Koreans, Americans who were posted in Korea were serving their personal ends. Most of them were building their reputations or fortunes, and recognized that a record of accomplishments could bring career advancement and additional income. Therefore they wanted successes, diplomatic victories, increased sales and profitable concessions, residence and travel privileges, converts, protection from local officials. As they sought these things, it helped to hint that favors granted to Americans would make the United States government more willing to back Korea against her enemies.

In 1887 King Kojong asked an American missionary, Dr. Horace N. Allen, how he could "interest the U.S. Governm't in Korea, and secure . . . help in keeping off China." The missionary answered, "Give the gold mining to an American company."[76]

Sixteen years later, Allen was still singing the same song, which had yielded a good return: the Unsan gold mine, a Seoul–

Chemulp'o railroad contract, and trolleys and electric lighting
in the Korean capital. Kojong (now emperor) again had a meeting with Allen, who had become the American minister to
Korea. In 1903 it was Japan, not China, that posed a threat to
Korean independence. If things got worse, what would the
Americans do? "Nothing" would have been a State Department
answer; instead, Minister Allen gave the old assurances. "I told
him that the United States was his friend, and that we were the
only people who could speak a strong and disinterested word
for him."[77]

It was not totally cold-blooded. Most members of the American community came to like the Korean people, in a conde-
scending fashion.[78] Some felt an attachment to Kojong and his
court, despite all the signs of weakness and corruption. Such
feelings, together with normal humanitarian impulses and dislike for aggression (aggression by *other* powers, anyway) produced a desire to help Koreans protect their dignity and independence. Besides, nearly all Americans believed it was their
duty to show humble people the proper path to progress and
Western ways.

The American community in Seoul knew that it was out in
front while the State Department was in retreat. Washington, in
its view, was wrong; a shift to a stronger policy would benefit
Korea, and United States interests generally. Therefore the
Americans in Seoul decided, and told their Korean contacts,
that they would try to turn things around, would attempt to
interest American officials back home in shifting from an inactive to an active policy.

And they *did* try. Members of the American community in
Seoul wrote to their friends in the States. They prepared arti-
cles and gave interviews about the stake of the United States in
Korea's future. When on home leave, they contacted their most
influential acquaintances, and tried their luck at lobbying in
Congress, at the State Department and the White House.

Their message was direct and clear. Switching from a hands-

off to a more active presence in Korea would pay off in trade
and concessions, in coaling stations if needed, and in an open
field for missionary operations. This, they pointed out, was in
line with the American nation's expansionist new world power
position of 1898. They noted that even without much State
Department help, the legation in Seoul and Americans outside
the legation had established a strong Christian presence in
Korea, had made trading gains, and had landed a few concessions. With Washington behind them, they could do much more.

It was a good try, but it did not work. The American community in Seoul did not have the strength or connections to carry
the day with the policymakers in Washington. Sometimes they
reached, but could not persuade, the important people. Often
they could not even reach the officeholders who made the key
decisions.

Under the then-prevailing system of political patronage,[79]
there was a fierce scramble for major diplomatic appointments;
but as Rockhill said, "Nobody wants Korea; it is too insignifi-
cant."[80] It was remote as well, and said to be dull and unheal-
thy;[81] and it was played down by the State Department.

As a result, the Seoul post went to minor figures who had
little influence in Washington and were not likely to be heard on
policy matters. Young party workers on the rise, or old politicians who rated an end-of-career assignment, were the usual
nominees.[82]

The story makes sad reading. The first minister, Lucius C.
Foote (1883–85), was a middle-level California politician with
Latin American experience but no important ties to President
Chester A. Arthur's Republican administration in Washington.
Democratic President Grover Cleveland's first minister to
Korea (William H. Parker, 1886) was a once-famous naval of-
ficer and writer who had a drinking problem. When he proved
to be too drunk to serve, he was replaced by a virtually un-
known young Arkansas lawyer, Hugh Dinsmore (1887–90). At
the same time, an incredible soldier of fortune, Charles Chaillé-

Long, was made legation secretary, he having been recommended by a Tammany gambler-politician.

After the Republicans won the 1888 election, President Benjamin Harrison appointed as minister a young Kentuckian, William O. Bradley, who had served his party in that Democratic state by taking eight successive beatings in election contests. Bradley refused to serve, so the job went to a retired China trader, Augustine Heard (1890–93). Then the Democrats returned, and Cleveland pleased a powerful Michigan Democrat by naming another retiree, an aging school superintendent, John M. B. Sill (1894–97).

None of these men had even visited Korea before they were given charge of the legation in Seoul. None pulled any weight in Washington, as Dinsmore, Heard, and Sill discovered when they recommended active policies.

Their successor, Dr. Horace N. Allen (minister 1897–1905), fell in a different category. He was an old Korean hand, having been the first Protestant missionary to establish residence in Seoul (1884). He could boast of diplomatic service with both the Koreans (on their mission to the United States, 1887–89) and the Americans (legation secretary under Heard and Sill, 1890–97). He had some grasp of the Korean language and was close to Kojong and others at court. What was more, his appointment owed less to politics than to the American businessmen he had assisted (with profit to himself). But like his predecessors, Allen lacked the political stature to influence decisionmaking in Washington. It was during his ministerial tenure that the United States government decided to abandon Korea.

American businessmen who made money in Korea also urged the United States government to increase its commitment to Korea. They too failed—mainly because, like their friends in the legation, they were small operators. Efforts to attract major financial figures, including Levi P. Morton, were unsuccessful (too small an opportunity and too many international complications). That left much of the action to such men as James R. Morse of the American Trading Company, and Henry Collbran and Harry Bostwick—capable people, but not rich enough to twist arms in Washington. Worse than that, they were so underfinanced that they were forced to sell out to the Japanese, wrecking Kojong's plan to use Americans to hold back Russia and Japan.

The colorful Leigh S. J. Hunt did a little better with his Unsan mine concession, and he had Washington connections, for Congressman J. Sloat Fassett was his associate. This, however, was not enough to change the policies of the United States government.[83]

The missionaries also did what they could. Their ties were with mission boards that were always assured of polite hearings in Congress, at the State Department, and at the White House. Besides, the boards and the individual missionaries had good business connections (the Reverend Horace G. Underwood, Presbyterian leader in Seoul, came from the typewriter family). But though deeply involved in Korean politics, the missionaries were reluctant to campaign in Washington. In any case, they were divided; prior to 1905 some thought a Japanese takeover would be good for Korea.[84] (The story of their later efforts appears in the following chapter, by Wi Jo Kang.)

Long before 1905, it had become apparent that Seoul's American community could not persuade the Washington authorities to share its enthusiasm for a stronger Korean policy. By continuing to raise Korean hopes, they did a disservice both to Korea and to the United States.

Conclusion

It was an unpleasant ending for what had been mostly an unpleasant story. The 1871 expedition was a failure. Then Li Hung-chang "opened" Korea to the United States, to balance

Russia and Japan. Instead, the Americans in Korea chose the other side. From 1883 to 1894, years of Chinese ascendancy, they opposed—rather ineffectively—Li's agent in Seoul, Yüan Shih-k'ai, and Yüan's conservative local allies.[85]

Lining up with Korea's pro-Japanese progressives, the Americans in the Korean capital became mired in factional politics, including Kim Ok-kyun's conspiracy in 1884.[86] This brought sharp reprimands from Washington; and from then on the State Department tried to curb the enthusiasm of its Seoul agents. This may have kept the American legation out of trouble, but sharply reduced its effectiveness and ability to help Korea.[87]

The situation did not improve when Japan ended China's domination of Korea at the end of the Sino-Japanese war (1895). When he was riding high, China's Yüan Shih-k'ai had been brutal, authoritarian, and anti-American. Viscount General Miura Gorō, Japan's new representative in Seoul, was worse on every count. He and his Korean allies (including the Taewŏn'gun, America's foe in 1871) introduced a reign of terror in 1895, murdering Queen Min and making King Kojong a virtual prisoner.

American diplomats, naval officers, advisers, and missionaries jumped into the fray, hoping to protect His Highness and to help what remained of the court's "American party." But again, the State Department rebuked its activist countrymen for interfering in Korean politics; and when Kojong fled from the palace in a humiliating coolie disguise, he went to the Russian, not the American, legation.[88]

During the ensuing period of Russian control (1896–98), the United States legation tried to work with the Russians and was rewarded by a grant of concessions to Americans. But then Chargé K. I. Waeber, who had worked with the Americans, was replaced by Alexis de Speyer, who wanted Kojong to "advise only with the Russians" and "put a cross" on the name of the head of the pro-American faction, Yi Wan-yong. Anti-American in general, because he wanted everything for Russia,[89] Speyer was particularly irritated by the Independence Club (1896–98). Run by Philip Jaisohn, a Korean-American adviser to Kojong, and supported by American missionaries and advisers, the club was anti-Russian as well as anti-Japanese. It was, in fact, in favor of Korea for the Koreans, and its demise (arranged by the Russians, the Japanese, and Korea's conservatives) was a setback for both the Korean independence movement and the United States.[90]

Russia presently pulled out; Speyer, like the American activists, had exceeded instructions from his government. This gave Japan a green light. Proceeding more cautiously than in 1895, the Japanese gradually increased their influence in Korea after 1898, completing the job by defeating Russia in the Russo–Japanese war in 1905. Some of the Americans in Korea resisted as best they could, but with little success. Finally, the whole game was lost when President Theodore Roosevelt gave way to the Japanese in a shockingly sudden fashion.[91] So it ended badly, with many Koreans convinced that they had been betrayed by the United States. Only American missionaries remained and, as Professor Kang demonstrates in the following chapter, continued the American influence in Korea in an unofficial way, to the consternation of Japan.

Very likely the outcome was inevitable,[92] given Korea's weakness and the probably wise determination of the American government to avoid involvement on the Asian mainland. Even so, it is unfortunate that the United States, having entered Korea on a trail of blood, should have professed friendship for twenty years, only to lead the Western parade in the 1905 withdrawal, which struck one American observer as "like the stampede of rats from a sinking ship."[93]

4

Relations between the Japanese Colonial Government and the American Missionary Community in Korea, 1905–1945

Wi Jo Kang

As Professors Lee and Harrington have demonstrated in previous chapters, Koreans could hardly rely on uninterested American government even before 1905. With conclusion of the Korean-Japanese Protectorate Treaty in 1905, Korea's sovereignty was lost (although official annexation of the country did not occur until five years later) and Japan took over the diplomatic and economic power of the Korean nation. As a result, there were no official Korean-U.S. relations to speak of from 1905 to 1945, except for the relationship between the American missionary community and the colonial Japanese government in Korea.

This missionary community in Korea provided a channel of information and communication for Koreans with the outside world, besides the official channels of the colonial government. In spite of the official missionary policies of noninvolvement in Korean politics and the neutral attitude of the missionary community toward Korean-Japanese relations, Koreans looked to the American missionary community for inspiration in the search for independence, and although many missionaries refused to become involved in the Korean independence movement, they were sympathetic with the cause. For example, on January 8, 1918, when President Woodrow Wilson announced the famous Fourteen Points, which included the doctrine of national self-determination, it was American missionaries who brought news of this principle to Korean Christian leaders. Although the missionary community generally remained neutral, the Japanese colonial government was aware of the potential power the community could wield against it. Thus the government was careful not to alienate the missionaries, and at certain times was even friendly with them.

However, the relationship was most often stressful and contentious, especially during World War II. In the early years of the war, the American missionary community strongly supported the Korean cause, and when the colonial government demanded that the community pay obeisance at Shinto shrines, as a sign of loyalty to Japan, most missionaries refused. Also, at the height of the war in the Pacific, Korea had no contact with the United States, except for a few Korean students who had been sent by American missionaries to the United States for advanced studies.

In many cases the missionary community in Korea was not welcome, and its relationship with the government often was not cordial. This essay examines the relationship between the American missionary community in Korea and the colonial government of Japan to shed light on these indirect Korean-U.S. relations between 1905 and 1945.

The Japanese Invasion and the American Missionaries

As the power of Japan grew in East Asia, Dr. Horace N. Allen, the first Protestant missionary to Korea, early recognized the threat to Korean independence that the Japanese posed.

Allen wished to save Korean independence and integrity from Japan's imperial ambition, evidenced by its increasing militarization.[1] He constantly warned his American superiors about the danger, but the information from Washington was always pro-Japanese, especially the news from President Theodore Roosevelt, who liked and often praised Japan. "Nothing in history has quite paralleled her rise during the last fifty years. Her progress has been remarkable alike in war, in industry, in statesmanship, in science."[2] Korea, as far as Roosevelt was concerned, "is absolutely Japan's."[3]

With this favorable view of Japan, held by the president of the United States, there was little hope for American assistance in maintaining Korean independence, although Allen complained to his government that such an attitude would only encourage a war that could ultimately harm the United States.[4] As Japan's growing power menaced Korean independence and freedom, Allen wrote a letter to Secretary of State John Hay, appealing on behalf of the Korean emperor and the relationship the two nations had once enjoyed with each other.[5] By this time, however, Allen's influence in Washington was slight, and his letter did not persuade anyone. At the 1905 Portsmouth Conference, which brought an end to the Russo-Japanese War, the neutrality of China was respected but Korean neutrality was ignored, and Japan's paramount interest in Korea was recognized by the American government and forced upon Russia. With that, there was almost no hope of maintaining Korean independence.

However, Allen did not cease his efforts for the Korean cause. He constantly reported Japanese activities to Washington and transmitted letters of protest from American residents in Korea (and Koreans themselves) against the Japanese. But very soon his support of Korean independence aroused the ire of the State Department, and in 1905 he was recalled to the United States and replaced by Edwin V. Morgan. Allen saw that he had little chance to win his fight for Korean sovereignty against the staunchly pro-Japanese public opinion in America.[6] Thus it was that the first Western nation to establish diplomatic relations with Korea was the first country to close its legation office and leave.

For the next forty years the only relations between the United States and Korea were indirect, with the Japanese colonial government through the American missionary community. For the most part, these missionaries were loyal citizens of their native land and therefore followed the foreign policy of the United States in regard to Korea. Besides, politics was not their major area of interest: "Nothing could be more uncalled for, or more injurious to our real missionary work, than for us to seem to take any part in the political factions of Korea."[7]

This policy of noninvolvement toward Korea's internal politics initially contributed to friendly and even cordial relations with the colonial government; the missionaries merely accepted the Japanese administration as the powers that be. This was clearly stated by the American board of the Presbyterian mission, the largest and most active missionary community in Korea: "Loyal recognition is, I believe, the sound position. It is in accord with the example of Christ, who loyally submitted himself and advised His apostles to submit themselves to a far worse government than the Japanese, and it is in line with the teaching of Paul in Romans xiii:*I.*"[8]

Conforming to this official decision, missionaries even advised Korean Christians to avoid political opposition to the Japanese, and according to Dr. Arthur Brown, secretary of the Board of Foreign Missions of the Presbyterian Church, the leaders of the Korean church unanimously accepted this position.[9] Consequently, if there were Korean Christians who tended toward anti-Japanese political action, they were kept from responsible positions in the church. Indeed, many Christian missionaries even welcomed Japanese rule. As one missionary wrote: "Prior to the annexation the administration system was chaotic. By stern enforcement the Japanese have introduced quiet and order, have commenced to exploit the natural resources of the country, set up a judiciary system, improved communication, and cultivated hygiene."[10] Dr. Brown was one of those who felt that the Japanese administration was an improvement over Korea's self-rule.[11]

The Conspiracy Case

It would seem, then, that there should have been no hostility by the Japanese colonial government toward the missionary community. However, Japanese authorities did not understand the spiritual nature of Christian activities in Korea and therefore suspected the Christian churches of being political agencies. This misinformed attitude resulted in fabrication of the so-called Conspiracy Case, so that in October 1911, Japanese police began to arrest leading Christian teachers and students in Seoul. Soon, Christian leaders in P'yŏngyang and Sŏnch'ŏn, areas where the Christian population was numerous, also were arrested. No explanation was given for these arrests, as more and more men were taken away.[12]

Finally, the administration accused Korean Christians of having plotted to assassinate Governor-General Terauchi as he passed through Sŏnch'ŏn in December of the previous year, and accused American missionaries of having provided pistols to carry out the plot. According to the 1912–13 report of the Japanese administration in Korea, the trial of a thief in Sŏnch'ŏn revealed the existence of conspirators intent upon assassinating Terauchi,[13] a "gang" that was purported to be Christian. Since the attempt was supposed to be made in Sŏnch'ŏn, arrests of Christians in that town were numerous.

The men who were accused in the Conspiracy Case were

students, officers, or pastors of Christian churches; and one of them was Baron Yun Ch'i-ho, a highly respected Christian leader. These men were imprisoned, without trial, until June 28, 1912, when 123 were indicted before the district court of Seoul. Newspaper accounts of the trial revealed startling travesties of justice, as well as the treatment of the individuals involved.[14] Throughout the trial, the men told of being tortured at the police station until they gave "confessions" of involvement in the alleged conspiracy.

One of the accused said he was tortured for four days. Another said: "I was bound up for about a month and subjected to torture. I still have the marks of it on my body." He asked permission to show evidence of the torture, but the court refused. Another man declared: "I was told by one of the officials that one man had been killed as a result of the torture, and I was threatened if I did not stick to the statements I had made, I should meet the same fate."[15] The falsity of these statements was plain to a long-time missionary who read the confession of an elder, who supposedly admitted (much to the missonary's surprise) that "several missionaries including myself had attended one of their meetings and had urged the Koreans to be brave and kill the Governor-General without fail. However, the record showed that the elder in his subsequent examination before the procurator had indignantly denied having had any part in or even knowledge of the alleged conspiracy."[16]

On September 28, when the trial came to an end, 105 men were found guilty. However, the sentences were very light, considering the seriousness of the accusation, and the court did not establish the guilt of the accused.

The entire trial was a fabrication, based upon hearsay and misinformation. For example, on the dates the prosecution charged Baron Yun with having met other plotters in Seoul, he was in Kaesŏng. Also, the forced confessions implied that 150 conspirators had made the trip to Sŏnch'ŏn to kill General

Terauchi at the end of December 1910, whereas the investigation showed that during the last six days of December the number of passengers who arrived in Sŏnch'ŏn, by two different railways, did not exceed 70. In addition, the trial involved no missionaries, who, if they *had* been at the meetings, and *had* supplied revolvers and "urged the Koreans to be brave and kill the Governor-General without fail," also should have been brought to trial. Since they weren't among the accused, the missionaries should have been allowed to testify on behalf of those who were, but the court refused to allow this.[17] The prosecutors of the "conspiracy" had no case, and the government was unable to produce the slightest evidence of conspiracy on the part of Christian leaders. The missionary community in Korea and the Christian churches in the United States that supported it were alienated from the Japanese by this mockery of justice.

The handling of the case was criticized from the beginning of the trial by missionaries and American legal specialists. The Japanese criminal code and the court procedure under which the Korean Christians were tried were criticized by missionaries as "archaic, barbaric, and uncivilized," and Dr. Charles Eliot of Harvard University, who was visiting Korea and Japan during the early investigations, advised the Japanese that their handling of the case was doing the nation harm.

> The two points I endeavored to make were, first, that no American would believe on any Korean evidence that a single American missionary was in the slightest degree concerned with the alleged conspiracy; and secondly, that the Japanese preliminary police investigation ought to be modified, and particularly, that counsel for the defense ought always to be present during all stages of the preliminary investigation. Counsel for the defense might or might not take part in the proceedings, but should invariably be present. I represented that the standing of Japan among Western nations would be improved by judicious modifications of her preliminary proceedings against alleged criminals.[18]

Since everything in the Conspiracy Case was published outside Korea, officials in the U.S. government gave the case "a
good deal of attention." In July 1912 a delegation, consisting of
Dr. Brown, Bishop Luther B. Wilson, Rev. Frank Mason North
(secretary of the Methodist Episcopal Board of Foreign Missions), and Dr. Edward F. Cook (secretary of the Board of Foreign Missions of the Methodist Church, South), visited Washington, D.C., to confer with the Japanese ambassador and the
American government regarding the situation in Korea.

> We told the Ambassador of our contemplated visit to our govern-
> ment regarding the Korean situation, in order that he might
> know directly from us, not only that we were going but what we
> were going for.
>
> From the embassy we went to the White House, where we
> were received with equal cordiality by President Taft. After a
> short conference with him, we went to the State Department,
> where Mr. Knox, the Secretary of State, spent a long time with
> us, going over the whole situation with painstaking care. . . .
>
> The interviews indicated that the responsible officials of our
> government had given a good deal of attention to the subject,
> that they had carefully read the documents that we had sent to
> them in advance, and that they had received voluminous infor-
> mation from other sources which they had studied with care.[19]

In Korea, many American missionaries saw the Conspiracy
Case as evidence of Japanese hostility toward and distrust of
the missionary community, and stated:

> We cannot be indifferent to the effect of the present policy of the
> Japanese police upon a mission work which now represents
> approximately 330 foreign missionaries . . . 500 churches, a
> Christian community of 250,000, property worth approximately
> a million dollars, and an annual expenditure of over $250,000.
> This extensive work is being injuriously affected by the reign of
> terror which now prevails among the Koreans.[20]

The Japanese administration was not pleased to hear such a
reaction, and on February 13, 1915, the colonial administration

decided to release all the "guilty" before the completion of their prison sentences. This event, nonetheless, unveiled to the missionary community an oppressive and hostile attitude of the Japanese administration toward Christians in Korea. Although the Conspiracy Case had been resolved, the Japanese authorities began openly to apply restrictive measures against missionary activities.

Restrictions on Medical Missionaries

The Japanese government was fully aware of the shortage of doctors in Korea and of the great assistance rendered by medical missionaries. Indeed, the need for doctors continued to be so great that the government permitted various Japanese to practice medicine without official license or qualification. Nevertheless, the medical practice of American missionaries was greatly restricted. On November 15, 1913, the governor-general issued an ordinance requiring all who desired to practice medicine to apply to him for permission, if they met these conditions:

1. those qualified according to the law in force in Japan;
2. those graduated from medical schools recognized by the governor-general;
3. those who had passed a medical examination prescribed by the governor-general;
4. those Japanese subjects graduated from medical schools of good standing in foreign countries;
5. those foreigners who have obtained a license in their respective countries, in which qualified Japanese subjects are permitted to practice medicine.[21]

Apart from the difficulties of obtaining a license under the requirements in items 1 through 4, item 5 made medical practice by American missionaries impossible in Korea, because only England permitted Japanese subjects, who had received medical training and certification in Japan, to practice medicine in England.

In October 1916 the first governor-general of Korea, Terauchi Masatake, left Korea to become premier of Japan and was replaced by another army general, Hasegawa Yoshimichi, who had been in Korea as commander in chief of the Japanese garrisons before the annexation. The new governor-general did not effect the slightest change in the policies established by General Terauchi; rather, he praised the administrative policies of his predecessor.[22] Part of the policies to be continued by the new administration were restrictive, aimed at missionary activities. As before, church services were infiltrated by the police, and missionaries were questioned about statements they made in sermons, making it clear that the Japanese colonial government persisted in its suspicion of Christian churches and the missionary community.

The Independence Movement and the Missionaries

On March 1, 1919, a nationwide independence movement was formed against the Japanese colonial government, and Korean Christians were participants. Sixteen of the thirty-three signatories of the new "Declaration of Independence" were Christian leaders, and many Christian churches became the gathering places of demonstrators for the reading of this declaration. As a result, the government blamed Christian missionaries for instigating this antigovernment movement. Many American missionary homes were searched, property was destroyed by the police, and some missionaries were attacked by soldiers and severely beaten. Under such conditions, the work of the church fell apart.

> Schools had to be closed, Bible classes could not be held, Bible Institutes could not finish, trips to the country had to be can-

celled, visiting in homes by missionaries was found to be inadvisable, many of our churches found their pastors, elders, helpers, and other church officers carried off to prison; missionaries lost their secretaries, language teachers, or literary assistants; every way we tried to turn regular work seemed impossible.[23]

Of all the repressive measures, the most tragic was the massacre of Christians in the village of Cheam-ni, south of Seoul. On April 16, 1919, Horace G. Underwood, the noted Presbyterian missionary, and some friends went visiting to Suŵon, near Cheam-ni. As they neared Suŵon they saw a large cloud of smoke, and Underwood questioned a neighboring farmer:

Underwood:	"What is that smoke?"
Farmer:	"That is a village that has been burned."
Underwood:	"When was it burned?"
Farmer:	"Yesterday."
Underwood:	"How was it burned?"
Farmer:	(glancing around fearfully) "By the soldiers."
Underwood:	"Why? Did the people riot or shout for independence?"
Farmer:	"No, but that is a Christian village."[24]

Later, in Cheam-ni, they learned that Japanese soldiers had arrived in the village the day before and had ordered all male Christians into the church. When about thirty had gathered, the soldiers fired on them with rifles, then killed the survivors with swords and bayonets, and then set fire to the church.

Such atrocities by the Japanese against Christians in Korea soon led to open hostility against the colonial government. Rev. Herbert Welch, bishop of the Methodist Episcopal Church in Korea, who had friendly contacts among high Japanese officials, visited Tokyo on his way to the United States and met with Prime Minister Hara Kei on May 15, 1919, to whom he expressed harsh criticism of Japanese activities in Korea.[25] The very next day, moreover, a committee of Christian missionaries from Korea visited Tokyo to report the oppressive situation in Korea to Japanese officials.

Missionaries took pictures of atrocities perpetrated on Korean Christians by Japanese soldiers and police, and spread the stories to the United States and Europe, in spite of efforts by Japanese authorities to conceal them through their control of the post offices, railroads, and press agencies. The Commission of Relations with the Orient of the Federal Council of Churches of Christ in America sent a cable to Premier Hara deploring the actions of the Japanese in Korea and demanding administrative reform.[26] In return, the commission received a conciliatory reply from the prime minister:

> I desire to assure you that the report of abuses committed by agents of the Japanese Government in Korea has been engaging my most serious attention. I am fully prepared to look squarely at actual facts. As I have declared on various occasions, the regime of administration inaugurated in Korea at the time of the annexation, nearly ten years ago, calls us for substantial modification to meet the altered conditions of things.[27]

At last, with the situation strained nearly to the breaking point, the Japanese government was about to improve its relations with the missionary community.

The Governmental Reform and Missionaries

On August 4, 1919, the Japanese government decided to replace the governor-general and introduce political reforms. The emperor appointed Admiral Saitō Makoto as the new governor-general on August 12, and a week later, on August 19, the "Imperial Rescript Concerning the Reorganization of the Government-General of Chōsen" was made public.

Quickly, the new administration tried to improve its relations with the missionary community. Soon after his arrival in Seoul,

Saitō met with representatives of the missionary community and asked them to express their frank opinions of the Japanese administration and to make suggestions. The Federal Council of Protestant Evangelical Missions in Korea prepared a statement and submitted it to Baron Saitō in September 1919. This statement, while expressing gratitude for the government's changed attitude, also blamed the Korean unrest upon the government's oppressive policies regarding religious freedom.[28]

The missionaries then urged that "religious liberty, which is already guaranteed by the constitution of the Empire of Japan, as of all other great nations, be made effective." Specifically, the missionaries requested (among other things) that they be allowed to teach the Bible in the church-school curriculum, that restrictions on use of the Korean language be removed, that teachers and pupils be allowed liberty of conscience, that hospital management be left to the staffs, and that censorship of Christian books be abolished.[29]

Subsequent meetings between government officials and missionaries were frequent. Before going to Korea, Dr. Mizuno, the new administrative superintendent, held a reception in Tokyo for prominent missionaries in Japan to become better acquainted with each other, in the hope of establishing better relations between the government and the missionaries in Korea.

The Saitō government soon modified the policies governing missionary work in Korea. Before reform, for example, permission from the governor-general was required for opening a new church, chapel, or other religious institution, and there was a stiff fine for noncompliance. In April 1920 the fine was abolished; church openings had only to be *reported* to the government. In addition, because the administration now wanted to recognize the contributions of the missionary community in Korea, the missionaries and the government maintained close contacts; and government officials often praised the missionary contribution toward the betterment of Korean life. At the tenth annual conference of the Federal Council of Protestant Evangelical Missions in Korea (Sept. 21, 1921), Dr. Mizuno stated:

> I have made several trips into the country, and the more familiar I become with the conditions in the peninsula, the more I do realize how painstakingly you labour for the uplift of the people. . . . It can be said without any appearance of flattery that Chōsen owes much of her advancement in civilization to your labours. . . . So we hold Christianity in high regard to give to it every possible facility for its propagation.[30]

The missionary community in Korea welcomed this improved relationship with the government, and took advantage of the new opportunities by holding many evangelistic campaigns and revival meetings.

In 1927 Governor-General Saitō left his post in Korea to attend the Geneva Disarmament Conference, but when he returned from Europe his health was failing and, on the advice of his doctor, he resigned the governor-general post. When the news of his resignation reached Korea, the executive committee of the Korean Mission of the Presbyterian Church in the United States sent a letter of appreciation to Baron Saitō for his friendly attitude toward the church, to which the baron responded with gratitude.[31]

In December 1927, General Yamanashi Hanzō was appointed governor-general. His policies followed those established by his predecessor, but his twenty-month term was too brief to bring about significant change. Then, surprisingly (in Aug. 1929), Baron Saitō was reappointed to his post in Korea and continued his friendly relationship with the missionaries. Unfortunately, his second term lasted only twenty-two months, and in June 1931 he was recalled to Tokyo.

General Ugaki Kazushige was appointed the new governor-general. Of course, the missionary community hoped that he

would continue the same relations which had existed under the
Saitō administration, and this desire was officially stated at the
Federal Council of Protestant Evangelical Missions meeting
(three months after the inauguration of the new governor). Initially, the Ugaki administration maintained conciliatory relations with the missionary community. Awards were even presented in recognition of the contribution by missionaries in
Korea. Dr. O. R. Avidson, a medical missionary and educator,
received the fourth degree of the Order of the Sacred Treasure
from the emperor of Japan, and early in 1937 the Imperial Educational Association presented Dr. Samuel Moffett with a gold
medal.

War Efforts, Shinto Issues, and the Missionary Community

In Tokyo, however, the political climate was changing. Militarists were expanding their influence and perpetrating ter-
rorist activities in order to suppress liberal, democratic
elements in Japanese politics. The militarists attacked Western
ideas of democracy and demanded chauvinistic devotion to the
emperor. Also, to make Koreans loyal subjects of the emperor,
the Japanese administration compelled all Koreans to participate in Shinto ceremonies, and new shrines appeared throughout the country where all Koreans were told to pay obeisance.

To the missionaries, this did not become a serious issue until
1935, when the government ordered all educational institutions,
including private Christian schools, to attend Shinto ceremonies. In previous years, whenever the government had asked
Christian schools to participate in Shinto ceremonies, these
schools had been able to participate in another form of patriotic activity. Now, however, the militarists had gained enough

strength in Japanese politics that their ideal of Shinto loyalism was the government's primary form of political control.

On November 14, 1935, the governor of South P'yŏngan Province called a meeting of all educators, including missionary educators, to enforce the policy of obeisance at Shinto shrines. Dr. George McCune, the president of Union Christian College in P'yŏngyang, and Miss Velma L. Snook, the principal of Sungŭi Girls' High School, refused to accede, and the governor ordered them to leave the meeting. But he gave them sixty days to reconsider. If the missionaries' attitude did not change, he said, their educational privileges would be revoked. When, after sixty days, the position of the missionaries remained unchanged, the government revoked the educational permits of McCune and Snook. In addition, McCune's house was watched by police and he was followed wherever he went. On January 20, 1936, Dr. McCune was relieved of the presidency of the college and Miss Snook of her position at the Sungŭi high school.

Missionaries who had encouraged Korean Christians to abandon their Confucian ancestor worship as idolatrous were not easily persuaded that paying obeisance to Shintoistic ancestral spirits was not a religious act. They continued to declare their loyalty to the Japanese government but believed that bowing to the shrines violated the First and Second Commandments, despite the government's insistence upon the nonreligious nature of Shinto ceremonies.

> We wish to express the high respect and loyalty which we hold toward His Imperial Majesty, the Emperor of Japan; this we do in gratitude for the blessing of good government. . . . But since we worship one God, alone, Creator and Ruler of the universe, revealed as the Father of Mankind, and because to comply with an order to make obeisance at shrines which are dedicated to other spirits, and at which acts of worship are commonly performed,

would constitute for us a disobedience to His expressed com-
mands, we therefore are unable ourselves to make such obeisance or to instruct our schools to do so.[32]

Opposition by the missionary community (especially the
Presbyterians) was so strong and the resulting tensions were so
great that the executive committee of the Board of Foreign
Missions of the Presbyterian Church in the United States recommended that the Korean mission schools be closed.[33] Thus,
the cordial relationship between American missionaries and
the Japanese government under Saitō's administration was
rapidly declining.

In August 1936 a tough-minded militarist, General Minami
Jiro, commander of the famous Kwantung Army, became governor-general of Korea, and with the approval of the militarist-
controlled Tokyo government, he placed Korea under a firm
military dictatorship. On July 7, 1937—less than a year after the
appointment of General Minami—shots were fired between
Japanese and Chinese soldiers at the Lukou-ch'iao, or Marco
Polo Bridge, and using this "China Incident" as a pretext, Japan
resumed war against China. As this war progressed, the Japanese made further efforts to separate American missionaries
from the Korean churches and to bring these churches under
the control of the church in Japan. Missionary activities that the
government disapproved became excuses for imprisoning or
expelling missionaries, and the Day of Prayer Incident, in September 1941, is a typical example.

In preparation for a World Day of Prayer, to be observed
during the last week of February by Christian women throughout the world, Miss Alice Butts (of P'yŏngyang) was asked by
Rev. Herbert Blair (chairman of the Federal Council of Churches) to make an outline of the Day of Prayer program available
to the churches. Upon examining this program, Japanese police
discovered a prayer "for the Peace of the World" and charged

that it was a sign of disloyalty to the war effort. Butts was imprisoned for a month and many Christian leaders were brought to police stations for interrogation.

Because of such incidents, the missionary community in Korea became completely subject to Japanese control, and the former cooperation was replaced by hostility and distrust. Missionaries could not hold meetings without police permission, and police representatives were required at all such meetings. American missionaries were not allowed to hold administrative positions in the church. Under such oppression, missionaries were compelled to withdraw from Korea. In October 1941 the U.S. consul-general, Gaylord March, informed mission representatives of a State Department order to evacuate all American missionaries, whereupon he brought the S.S. *Mariposa* to Inch'ŏn harbor, and on November 16 practically all American missionaries were evacuated.

Conclusion

Overall, relations between the Japanese colonial government and the American missionary community were distrustful and unfriendly (despite the brief period of cordiality under the administration of Saitō). Although the missionaries recognized the Japanese government as "the powers that be," and even went so far as to praise the alien government, the Japanese government distrusted their intentions. After the evacuation from Korea, American missionaries desired only the defeat of the enemy, Japan, and to return to Korea. When Korea was liberated, the returning missionaries started a new page that has made lasting marks on U.S.-Korean relations in the post–World War II period.

5

Transition and Continuity in American-Korean Relations in the Postwar Period

Robert T. Oliver

The relationship of the United States and the Republic of Korea following Pearl Harbor illustrates how a continuing policy is subject to recurrent transitional shocks. Essentially, the friendship expressed by America toward Korea in earlier periods has not only continued, but has been manifested through significant diplomatic, economic, and military measures. In the immediate postwar period, this relationship became much more complex than in the period immediately preceding (1905–45), which, as Professor Kang has shown, was unofficial yet friendly, carried on by American missionaries.

The Republic of Korea was established by U.S. initiative. The invasion from the north was beaten back under American leadership. Devastated South Korea was rehabilitated largely with American economic aid. South Korea, on the other hand, has done more than its share as a bastion of defense against further Communist advance in Northeast Asia. It has developed sufficient economic, diplomatic, and military resources to be a valuable ally. The bonds between the two countries are closely knit;

but there have been sharp differences, with disappointments felt keenly by both sides.

A pattern to these differences was established early, and generally passed through three phases. The first, from January 1942 through December 1945, was marked by the formulation of American policies toward Korea. The second phase was dominated by the Cold War between the United States and Russia. The third phase was that of United Nations involvement in Korea. Through all of them, the basic policy of friendly alliance was maintained, though frequently disturbed by severe shocks. The strength of the ties that bind the two countries together can best be estimated by considering the disappointments and difficulties that had to be surmounted.

Phase One: Development of Policies toward Korea

In mid-August 1945, as Japan was toppling in surrender, jubilation spread through the Korean populace. The surrender meant that the independence of their nation, lost for a generation, would be restored. It also meant that they would once more have schools, newspapers, books, and could converse with their neighbors in their own language. They would no longer be required to use "Japanized" names, nor render obeisance at Shinto shrines, nor hail the emperor of Japan as their overlord. They would be enabled to return to being Korean. The products of their labor would be their own. After four decades of enforced Japanization, they would be free again, as their ancestors had been for thousands of years.

Then came the news of Russian troops entering their country in the north and of American troops in the south, dividing their country in two. Foreboding replaced exhilaration. As days, weeks, and months passed, dismay darkened the people's expectations. When Japanese-run mines, factories, and businesses were closed, unemployment sharply increased. With transportation and commodity markets disrupted, food became scarce and prices shot upward. The division quickly proved to be tragic, not only for Korea but also for the world.

How the division of Korea came about is a study in diplomatic bungling. The responsibility rests, first of all, upon President Franklin D. Roosevelt. As the leader of the Allied coalition, his twofold aims were to win World War II and to establish postwar conditions that would lead to lasting peace. In his view, both these problems converged around Allied relations, and especially those between the United States and Soviet Russia. He sought ways to unite these two basic aims.

The Pearl Harbor attack had not only precipitated the United States into the war but also initiated a Japanese advance throughout the South Pacific. Looking beyond the series of dismal defeats that marked 1942, Roosevelt searched for a plan that would bring Russia into the Pacific War and that would cement a lasting alliance through establishment of the United Nations. To accomplish both aims, he felt it was necessary to accept Russia's entrance into both Eastern Europe and Korea.

The unfolding of American policies toward Korea began in January 1942. The Pacific War Council decided that an immediate promise to restore Korea's independence would be "premature and unwise."[1] Instead, Roosevelt's policies followed a course that was, on the surface, idealistic, but essentially expedient—a combination not unusual for leaders conducting a major war. Echoing Woodrow Wilson, Roosevelt's peace aims included "self-determination of nations and peoples." But, like Wilson, he only partially meant what he said, and—as Wilson had—he excluded Korea from the formula.

Unknown to Korea and the world, decisions were made that led inexorably to the 1945 division of Korea. In the Department of State, a study group proposed that, after the war, Korea be placed under an international trusteeship. On March 27, 1943,

Roosevelt suggested that idea to Anthony Eden, the British foreign secretary, and in October of that year he repeated it at the Quebec Conference with Winston Churchill.[2] It seems clear why (in the words of Cordell Hull) he "enthusiastically" pursued this idea. He needed to get Russia into the war and he knew of the Russian desire for Korea's all-year warm-water seaports. For the long term, Russian cooperation would be required to maintain a stable peace, and Russian participation in a four-power trusteeship over Korea would be a beginning in teamwork. Roosevelt believed the Korean people were unprepared for self-government, and he had the example of American trusteeship over the Philippines as a transitional step toward eventual independence.

From this genesis, the division of Korea became inevitable. "Unilaterally"—in the later judgment of a sixteen-year veteran of the U.S. Foreign Service—"we proposed the August, 1945, division of Korea, knowing that any 'temporary' division with the Soviets was like a little pregnancy."[3] However, there seems little reason to believe that the *lasting* division of Korea was foreseen, let alone planned. But there is every reason to think that the delivery of at least northern Korea into the Soviet sphere of influence became, in 1943, an essential part of American foreign policy. No doubt Roosevelt felt that delay in Korean independence was a small price to pay for the peace system he envisioned.

Disunity within the Korean nationalist movement overseas provided an excuse for Roosevelt's decision. Just two weeks after the Pearl Harbor attack, he instructed Clarence Gauss, the American ambassador in Chungking, to investigate the status of the Korean Provisional Government, and his report provides a startling view into the thinking that governed American foreign policy. The Korean Provisional Government, Gauss said, was dominated by moderates and was not supported by the

Communist National Revolutionary Party, which was comprised of Korean Communists in Manchuria. Consequently, it was deemed unsuitable for recognition.

In a further move to determine the worth of the expatriate Korean resistance movement, Roosevelt asked T. V. Soong, China's ambassador to Washington, to determine the representative character of the exiled independence group. Soong's deputy, Victor Hoo, talked with Syngman Rhee and urged him to form a coalition with Kilsoo Han, who was at the time a favorite of officials in the lower echelon of the Far Eastern Division of the State Department. Dr. Rhee, citing Han's presumed relations with the radical Black Dragon Society in Japan, refused. Ambassador Soong then reported to Roosevelt that the Koreans were hopelessly divided.[4]

Shortly after the Pearl Harbor attack, Dr. Rhee asked Senator Guy Gillette to help persuade the State Department to support Korean independence. On December 8, 1941, Gillette wrote to Rhee that "I have discussed the recognition of Korea as an independent entity with the State Department. I found them sympathetic but of course no action can be taken. . . . You can readily see that we could not and should not take any steps to arouse resentment which might find expression in abuse or misuse of Americans still resident in the Japanese Empire." Rhee went at once to the senator's office, where the same sentiments were repeated. "In that case," Dr. Rhee told him, "the war is lost. How can you fight a war without offending the Japanese?" Senator Gillette replied: "I have but told you what the State Department said."[5]

Dr. Rhee found a more sympathetic attitude in the Department of War. However, the most he could secure from government officials was a ruling by the Department of Justice that Koreans in America who had not registered as Japanese citizens would be accorded special status as "Korean nationals." Rhee's appeal for Lend-Lease aid was fruitless. "Disillusionment with the West, therefore," a leading Korean historian of the period has noted, "led many young intellectuals and other nationalists in Korea to look to the Soviet Union."[6]

In late November 1943, Roosevelt, Churchill, and Chiang Kai-shek met in Cairo to coordinate their Asian war aims. The generalissimo proposed that they issue a promise that "Korea shall be free and independent." Roosevelt reminded the other leaders of his plans for a trusteeship and, with Churchill's support, the declaration was amended by addition of the phrase "in due course."[7] Rhee promptly wrote to Secretary Hull for clarification of the intent of the phrase but received no reply.[8]

For the next two years there were no overt policy acts relative to Korea. Allied attention was centered on Europe and Africa. Moreover, Allied unity was threatened by Stalin's demands for an attack across the English Channel to relieve pressure on his defensive positions. Instead, North Africa was invaded. In February 1945, when the leaders met at Yalta, Roosevelt offered a "policy guide" which included the startling proposition: "The position of the Soviet Union in the Far East is such that it would seem advisable to have Soviet representation on an interim international administration of Korea regardless of whether or not the Soviet Union enters the war in the Pacific."[9]

Public opinion in the United States concerning Roosevelt's design for strengthening American-Soviet relations was mixed. Sumner Welles, in his syndicated newspaper column, wrote: "With the restoration of Korean independence, one of the great crimes of the twentieth century will have been rectified, and another stabilizing factor will have been added to the new international system which must be constructed in the Pacific." Other commentators, however, favored the Rooseveltian view of appeasement of Russia. Wendell Wilkie wrote: "Russia is an effective society. It works. . . . Russia is our ally in this war. . . . We must work with Russia."[10] Senator Arthur Vandenberg also

endorsed the Rooseveltian peace formula.[11] *Time* magazine
featured a picture of Stalin, captioned "Uncle Joe," on its cover.
Eleanor Roosevelt tried to persuade her husband to grant
Korean nationalists Lend-Lease aid, but without success.[12]

Roosevelt's design to placate Russia, in order to win its cooperation, had a measure of plausibility and he held to it. It was
only later (*too* late) that George F. Kennan reminded Americans
that Russia "is by far the weaker party" and urged resistance to
Soviet domination of its bordering nations.[13] American policy
toward Asia was depicted in two popular phrases: "trade space
for time" and "wait for the dust to settle."

At the Potsdam Conference, in July 1945, President Harry
Truman agreed that northern Korea might be occupied by Russian troops and that a four-power trusteeship should be established over the peninsula. The subsequent acceptance of the
38th parallel as the line of demarcation came in General Douglas MacArthur's General Order Number One, after Japan's defeat. In October, John Carter Vincent first revealed to the public
the long-pending plan for trusteeship.[14] Two months later, when
the Allied leaders met in a stormy conference in Moscow, the
discussion concerning Korea erupted in bitter disagreement. As
the historian Lisle A. Rose described it, when Secretary of State
James Byrnes "turned to the issue of Anglo-American-Soviet
establishment of a joint trusteeship over Korea . . . and asked
Molotov why the Russians were refusing to help in the establishment of a unified transportation and postal service for the
peninsula, the foreign minister became so evasive and the hour
so late that the discussion was postponed."[15] The question of
coordination of the two military zones was never resolved. Nevertheless, the trusteeship plan was announced, on December
27.

Perhaps American officials failed to understand Russia's plan
for Korea; or they may have sensed it but had gone ahead
anyway. In either event, "it wasn't many weeks after the

Moscow Conference before nearly everyone who had anything
to do with the Moscow Declaration deeply and honestly regret-
ted it."[16] Korean nationalists regarded the trusteeship an-
nouncement as "a shocking fact that stems from an erroneous
perception of Korean realities and ignores the people's will."[17]
State Department officials soon sought ways of withdrawing
from the trusteeship commitment. Byrnes tried to reassure the
Korean people by declaring that "it is our goal to hasten the day
when Korea will become an independent member of the society
of nations."[18]

In historical perspective, we know that the trusteeship plan
was fatally flawed. Even in the Philippines, where trusteeship
was supervised by only one power, it had lasted a full generation. Inevitably, the Four Power plan for Korea would have
given the Soviet Union predominant control, because the
United States was anxious to withdraw from the Asian conti-
nent; Nationalist China was far too weak to exercise much
influence; and Great Britain had for many years favored Japanese or Chinese control over Korea, had no immediate interest
in Korea's future, and was fully occupied with recovering from
its losses in the war. The Soviet Union alone was determined to
"impose its . . . social system" over Korea. In its view, trusteeship was merely a transitional step toward such control.[19]
Korea, divided under two sets of military government, was
without resources, internal strength, and Allied support. Even
so, through sturdy resistance its patriot leaders defeated the
trusteeship plan. But they were unable to end the division that
tore their land apart.

Phase Two: The Cold War

During the three-year period following the defeat of Japan,
Big Power rule over Korea was neither realistic nor politic. A

Cold War quickly developed, scuttling Roosevelt's grand design for Soviet-American cooperation. Among Korean leaders who sought a solution for their country, unity was prohibited by ideological and practical divisions that could not be surmounted. One group formed the Democratic Party, under the leadership of the newspaper *Dong-A Ilbo* editorial board: Kim Sŏng-su, Song Chin-u, and Chang Taik-sang, all of whom had been educated in Japan. All were well versed in English and well informed concerning international relations. Their convictions were strongly anti-Communist and socially and economically conservative.

A second group was led by Yŏ Un-hyŏng (also known as Lyuh Woon-hyong), who had been selected by the Japanese governor-general (on August 14, 1945) to head the Committee for the Establishment of the Korean State. With a long record as a nationalistic Communist, he had been prominent in the struggle to extricate Korea from the control of Japan. On September 6, Yŏ convened a conference of leftist leaders from the various provinces and proclaimed creation of the People's Republic (with a 55-member legislature)—on the day before the arrival of the first American troops. Syngman Rhee, who was still in America, was named president, but the executive authority was to be exercised by a Communist prime minister, Hŏ Hŏn. In the cabinet, all the vice-ministers, who would have the administrative functions, were Communists. The funds with which this group operated came from North Korea and its program probably was directed by the Soviet consulate-general, which was the only Allied diplomatic office in Seoul.

General John R. Hodge, commander of the American occupation forces, immediately disavowed this self-proclaimed "government." The non-Communist members promptly resigned and gave their allegiance to Kim Sŏng-su's Democratic Party, which chose Rhee as its chairman and pledged its support to the Korean Provisional Government, still headquartered in Chungking.

A third domestic group was led by Pak Hŏn-yŏng, who was released from a Japanese jail on August 16 and promptly proclaimed reestablishment of the Korean Communist Party. With credentials from Moscow, Pak called for a "bourgeois democratic revolution" and began a campaign of propaganda and organization throughout South Korea. For a year he enjoyed full freedom, but on September 16, 1946, when a money-printing press was found in his headquarters, he was charged with the crime of counterfeiting, but was able to flee to North Korea. In 1955 he was charged with treason, as a spy for the United States, and (as a "revisionist") was executed.

A fourth nationalist group was led by An Chae-hong, an educator and journalist with a record of courageous anti-Japanese activities. He cooperated closely with the American military authorities and was named administrator of civilian affairs under the occupation.

The three most prominent expatriate leaders were Dr. Syngman Rhee, who arrived in Seoul on October 16 from America, and Kim Ku and Kim Kyu-sik, who arrived on November 23 from Chungking. Dr. Rhee's return created the most excitement. As recorded by Richard D. Robinson, Rhee "had one big advantage; either through design or historical accident, his name was the most revered and respected among the Korean villagers. In the minds of the people he occupied a place somewhat akin to that of a legendary hero."[20] It soon became a major theme of Communist propaganda, that Rhee was "an American puppet," but an official history of the American Military Government in Korea noted Rhee's return in unfriendly terms: "It is clear that the State Department had doubts as to Rhee's value in bringing order to the excited political scene there. He had been a steady critic of the department and U.S. policies, and furthermore he was in his seventieth year and had been away from his homeland for many years."[21]

Dr. Rhee at once commenced a campaign to renounce trusteeship and to build anti-Communist sentiment in South Korea. On November 21 he shocked General Hodge by a radio speech in which he denounced communism as the worst enemy of the Korean people. On December 16 he organized the Economic Contributors' Association to raise funds for developing an independent Korean policy. In June 1946, General Hodge told an American visitor: "Dr. Rhee is so much the greatest of Korean statesmen that I could almost say he is the only one. But he can never have any place in a Korean government unless he stops his attacks upon Communism."[22] As a final comment upon Communist depiction of Rhee as an American puppet, General Hodge wrote to an American senator (Brian McMahon, on February 2, 1948) that "Dr. Rhee has not been for over a year, and is not now, working in cooperation with the United States to bring forth an independent Korea, but actually is making our task more difficult. He has done much in the past year to bring about distrust by the Koreans of the Occupation Forces and of United States policies."[23]

Dr. Rhee's policies were spelled out by his American spokesman in the *New York Times* on November 10, 1946:

> We should disband our American Military Government in Korea and set up a genuine Korean government south of the 38th parallel in its place. We should leave troops there, under the command of General John R. Hodge, as a barrier to further Russian aggression against Korea. We would make every effort available to us to force Russia to keep her promise of withdrawing from northern Korea, so the country can be reunited. We should sponsor the admission of Korea to the United Nations so it can plead its own cause. We should at once exempt Korea from the restrictions applying to Japan. We should set up Korean currency on the international exchange, so that imports will be possible. And we should aid materially in rehabilitating the economy of South Korea so that a decent prosperity can be developed there.

During 1946–47, the real contest for Korea was between the United States and the Soviet Union. While Russia systematically converted the north into a puppet state, the American Military Government tried to implement the Moscow trusteeship agreement. Rhee and Kim Ku, at the same time, insisted upon election of a Korean government in the south that would be a fully independent and democratic all-Korea government. Curiously, while the Cold War evolved into the hostility that culminated in the Berlin Blockade, American policy in South Korea was to renounce anticommunism, in an effort to secure Soviet agreement to the trusteeship that virtually all Koreans—Communists included, until Moscow forced them to change—refused to accept.

In 1947 the triumvirate of returned expatriate leaders—Rhee, Kim Ku, and Kim Kyu-sik—separated and formed three contending groups. Rhee formed the Society for the Immediate Establishment of Korean Independence, to demand the prompt holding of an election to form an interim government that would negotiate to end the division and lay the basis for a reunified state. Kim Ku demanded recognition of the exiled Korean Provisional Government. Kim Kyu-sik worked closely with the American Military Government, in the hope that an American-Soviet agreement might reestablish Korean unification. To this end, he joined Yŏ Un-hyŏng to form a Coalition Committee and became the unofficial American choice for the Korean presidency when a government was established.[24]

The despair felt by Korean nationalists was well expressed by Pyŏn Yŏng-t'ae in the July 7, 1947, issue of *Dong-A Ilbo*:

> Both the Russian military command in North Korea and the American military command in South Korea have one thing in common. Their activities are consistently and persistently directed toward crushing Korean nationalism. . . . We readily understand the Russians, their aim is so transparent, that of removing the one paramount obstacle that stands in the way of Sovietizing Korea. But we can only open our mouths wide in astonishment at the doings of the American military authorities,

intended to sap, dispirit, and adulterate the nascent, bewildered
Korean national sentiment, for they are generally supposed not
to subsidize Communism. Still, that is exactly what they are
doing—all that most sanguine Communists can ever expect
their professed political antagonists to do in advancing the Red
cause itself.

In similar resentment, Colonel Ben C. Limb, a lifelong leader
in the independence movement, wrote in a private letter:

Looking realistically at the present situation of Korea, what
should the Korean people do? Americans berate them for their
dislike of Communism, and tell them they must learn to live
happily with the Russians. In the final analysis, perhaps this is
correct. If America will not stand by its commitments to Korean
independence—if the United States treats Korea primarily as a
bargaining item that may perhaps be profitably traded off for
advantages elsewhere—then the proper course for Korea becomes clear. We shall be forced to change horses in the middle
of the stream. We shall be forced, though much against our will,
to work out our destinies as a people within the Soviet sphere.[25]

The development that caused the long-smoldering dismay of
Koreans to burst forth in such bitter statements was the recon-
vening in Seoul (May 21, 1947) of the U.S.-U.S.S.R. Joint Commission. Kim Kyu-sik, supported by leftists and moderates,
formed the National Independence Federation to promulgate
the thesis that the nation could be reunited, and even be independent, through American-Russian cooperation. Therefore,
the first duty of patriotic Koreans was whatever was needful to
bring them into accord.

Kim Kyu-sik, Yŏ Un-hyŏng, and all the leftist groups in South
Korea, with the Communist regime in the north, welcomed resumption of the trusteeship discussions. The rightists, led by
Syngman Rhee, Kim Ku, and Kim Sŏng-su, opposed them, as did
the bulk of the population. Then came a Soviet-American agreement that the Joint Commission would limit its hearings to

Koreans who agreed, in writing, to endorse the trusteeship plan. This decision was announced on June 12. Very soon, its condemnation throughout South Korea convinced the United States that this exclusion was a mistake. On August 26 the State Department urged Moscow to agree to nationwide elections of a provisional government. When the Soviets replied that the trusteeship plan must, instead, be implemented, Secretary of State George Marshall (on September 17) asked the General Assembly of the United Nations to place the "Korean problem" on its agenda. Marshall supported his request by saying that "we do not wish to have the inability of two powers to reach an agreement delay any further the urgent and rightful claims of the Korean people to independence."[26]

The General Assembly agreed, by a vote of 41 to 6 (with 7 abstentions), to consider the Korean question. By this action the problem of the status of Korea was taken out of the bilateral Soviet-American context (China and Great Britain had played no significant role in the policy formulation) and became the responsibility of the United Nations. The Cold War continued to be the chief determinant in the decision-making process, but the forum was broadened and the issues no longer revolved on "what had been agreed to in the Moscow Conference of December, 1945," but "what next should be done."

Phase Three: United Nations Involvement

By 1947 it had become evident that the wartime alliance which defeated the Berlin-Rome-Tokyo Axis had dissolved into confrontation between systems represented by the United States on one side and the Soviet Union on the other. Weak though the United Nations inevitably had to be, it provided at least a hope of avoiding the catastrophe of another world war, and the Korean question became a focal point of Russian-Amer-

ican policy differences. As a historian of the period notes, "Ultimately, the unification issue hinges on the basic questions of
who would control the government of a united Korean state,
and what its political and social structure would be."[27]

The Soviet Union presented a proposal to the General Assembly that all foreign troops be withdrawn from Korea, with
the problems besetting the peninsula to be left to the inhabitants. Since Russia had organized the North Korean regime and
supplied it with a well-trained and well-equipped army, and
since the United States had kept South Korea disorganized,
with no military force except a small constabulary for police
duties, it was obvious that withdrawal of the American troops
would result in surrendering the whole of Korea to Communist
control. The United States rejected the Russian proposal, on
the grounds that the status of foreign troops was an "integral
part" of the Korean problem and should be determined after,
not before, a general settlement. Supported by what Russia
termed an American "automatic majority" in the United Nations, the General Assembly accepted the U.S. recommendation
to create a United Nations Temporary Commission on Korea
(UNTCOK), charged "to insure that the Korean representatives
will in fact be duly elected by the Korean people and not mere
appointees from military authorities in Korea."

When the American plan was accepted, Andrei Gromyko, the
Soviet delegate, warned that "the U.S.S.R. would not be able to
take part in the work of the Commission."[28] Nevertheless, on
November 17 the UNTCOK was formally established. The resolution further called for holding elections not later than March
31, 1948, under supervision of the commission, which was to be
composed of representatives of Australia, Canada, China, El
Salvador, France, India, the Philippines, Syria, and the Ukraine.
After the Ukraine refused to participate, the remaining eight
delegates divided into two groups, with Australia, Canada, and
India generally favorable to a compromise based upon a coali-

tion equally representative of North and South, whereas the others favored a free electoral choice by the predominantly non-Communist population. The General Assembly set up an Interim Committee (popularly called the Little Assembly) to supervise implementation of such a plan as would emerge "in the light of developments." The prospects were not auspicious. Russia had made it clear that it would not accept U.N.-sponsored elections in the North. But the resolution had made no provision for a separate election in the South, nor was there any indication of what, if any, Korean groups would be consulted.

In January 1948, when the commission assembled in Seoul, it quickly found that it could not operate in the North; so it referred the problem back to the Little Assembly. The Soviet Union denounced UNTCOK as "a puppet consisting of the henchmen of American imperialism whose object is to make a colony of Korea," and rallies were held throughout North Korea "in opposition to . . . elections for the formation of a reactionary separate government in South Korea."[29] Kim Ku also opposed the U.S. plan as "foreign intervention" and called, instead, for recognition of his Korean Provisional Government. Kim Ku then joined with Kim Kyu-sik to accept the North Koreans' call for a "South-North Political Consultative Conference," which would create a "democratic state" for a reunited nation. The North Korean Communists, on April 19, assembled 695 delegates (alleged to represent all segments of Korean opinion) to convene in P'yŏngyang.

When Kim Ku and Kim Kyu-sik arrived, they found that resolutions already had been prepared and that they were expected to be mere observers. On April 30, the conference called for withdrawal of all foreign troops and for a subsequent conference to draft a constitution for the new state. Returning to Seoul, Kim Kyu-sik confessed the failure of the unity effort and withdrew from politics. Kim Ku, in contrast, reported that he

had found the Communist leader, Kim Il-sung, conciliatory toward the rightists and he urged that the public support the
P'yŏngyang resolution.

Syngman Rhee, insisting that he wished to "implement the
U.N. Commission," pointed out that it had no representative
body of Koreans with whom to consult and, accordingly, proposed an immediate election in the south to provide a body
equivalent to the regime already existing in the north. He was
deeply suspicious that the commission would favor a "coalition" solution, and his suspicions were confirmed. On January
12, India's K. P. S. Menon, as chairman of UNTCOK, told an
assembly in Seoul that "independence is not enough. There
must be unity." Both Kim Ku and Rhee walked off the platform,
and Police Chief Cho Pyŏng-ok heatedly told Menon that
"Korea is on the verge of a breakdown, political, social, and
economic, because the flower of liberty has not yet borne
fruit."[30]

The UNTCOK report to the Little Assembly led to a vote (31
to 2) to hold elections "in such parts of Korea as are accessible
to the Commission." General Hodge announced that the election would be in May (May 10), and it resulted in an overwhelming victory for the rightists. On July 12 a constitution "for all
Korea" was adopted, and on July 20 Dr. Rhee was elected president of the Republic of Korea, by a vote in the National Assembly of 180 for him and 13 for Kim Ku. North Korea countered by
inaugurating (Sept. 9) the Democratic People's Republic of
Korea, with Kim Il-sung its president. In November, the United
Nations (meeting in Paris) recognized the Republic of Korea as
the legitimate government, chosen by the people, and "as the
only such government in Korea." Russia and the Soviet bloc
promptly recognized the Northern regime, and the United
States and other anti-Communist nations recognized the Southern government. Somberly, the Koreans realized that they were
"Korean" no longer; they were, instead, either "South Korean"

or "North Korean." During June and July 1949, the United States
withdrew the last American troops from South Korea, and one
year later, on June 25, 1950, North Korea launched a well-pre-
pared but surprise invasion of the South.

Responsibility for that attack has been much discussed.[31]
Russia contributed to it by building a strong military force in
North Korea and by insisting that the people of South Korea
longed to escape from their "puppet dictatorship," to join with
their Northern brethren in the "democracy" of the People's Re-
public. China must have shared in the preparations, for it
moved its best battle-ready troops toward the Manchurian-
Korean border just before the invasion. During the spring of
1950, the United States no doubt encouraged the Communists
to anticipate success in statements by Secretary of State Dean
Acheson, Senator Tom Connally, and General Douglas Mac-
Arthur, all insisting that America's "perimeter of defense" in
Asia did not include the Korean peninsula. President Syngman
Rhee, although he has been blamed for his threats to reunite
Korea by force, some three and a half months before the inva-
sion wrote an anguished apprehension that an attack was
imminent:

> You can gain some appreciation of our position if you consider
> that we are sitting here in Seoul, knowing that the enemy in the
> North can sweep down on us at any moment with more arms,
> more planes, more of everything than we can muster against
> them. We have no anti-aircraft guns, no planes we can put in the
> air at the present time, not even any ammunition.

He blamed the State Department for blocking development of a
South Korean defensive force, from fear that to do so "might
aggravate relations with Russia."[32]

After the invasion, President Truman was assured by John
Foster Dulles, U.S. Ambassador John Muccio, and a field team
of the United Nations (all of whom had direct knowledge of

conditions south of the 38th parallel) that the Republic of Korea had made no preparations for defense of the border, let alone an attack across it. In deciding to defend South Korea and to ask the United Nations to sponsor the defense, Truman made it very clear that his purpose was not to "save" South Korea but to prohibit Communist forces from making gains through military aggression. He called the U.N.-U.S. intervention a "police action" and proclaimed that "victory is not our aim." As he wrote in his memoirs, "Every decision I made in connection with the Korean conflict had this one aim in mind: to prevent a third world war and the terrible destruction it would bring to the civilized world."[33]

The war aims of the United States and the Republic of Korea, however, were significantly different. The U.S. aim was simply to discourage Communist aggression; the ROK aim was to reunite the severed nation. After the success of the Inch'ŏn landing in routing North Korean forces from the South, the United Nations defined its aims in consonance with the Republic of Korea. In a General Assembly resolution of October 7 it authorized General MacArthur to advance into the North to fulfill its commitment to reestablish a freely elected democratic government over the reunited peninsula. After the entry of Chinese forces into the conflict, this U.N. commitment was abandoned, though never disavowed. The result was a truce that left the Communist regime in control of the North, while reaffirming the U.N. determination to find a peaceful way of reuniting the country.[34]

Even though the United States was involved in the Korean War as only one of sixteen member-nations of the United Nations, it played the dominant and most important role. Following the truce in 1953, Washington continued to dominate the military, economic, and political affairs of the Republic of Korea. After the war was over, the sixteen nations that had participated on the side of South Korea, under the United Nations, signed the Declaration Concerning the Korean Armistice and pledged to resume fighting against the aggressor if military attack were renewed. Moreover, in view of the strong desire on the part of President Syngman Rhee and his people for unification of the two Koreas under a pro-Western regime, the Eisenhower administration signed the United States-Republic of Korea Joint Statement of August 7, 1953, promising to "consult further regarding the attainment of a united, free, and independent Korea."

Furthermore, in spite of the fact that the Republic of Korea declined to be a signatory to the Korean armistice of 1953, the United States and South Korea concluded a Mutual Security Pact in 1954, providing that each nation "would act to meet the common danger in accordance with its constitutional process." In addition to this alliance, Washington throughout the 1950s and 1960s sent a great amount of economic and military aid to South Korea. Having utilized American aid prudently, South Korea, which had been characterized as "a hopeless and bottomless pit" in the early 1950s,[35] by the 1970s became "a shining example among the success stories of U.S. aid programs to less developed countries after World War II."[36]

Most South Koreans recognize the vital role the United States has been playing in the modernization, industrialization, and militarization of their country. However, the intensity of the American commitment to the security of South Korea vis-à-vis North Korea has been uncertain. South Koreans have been aware of the different intensity in the American commitment to members of the North Atlantic Treaty Organization and to their country, as expressed by the 1954 Mutual Security Pact. Nevertheless, throughout the Eisenhower, Kennedy, Johnson, Nixon, and Ford administrations the South Koreans felt confident about American commitment jointly to defend their country in another North Korean attack. However, their confidence in an American response began to be shaken when, on December 21, 1976, President-elect Jimmy Carter made the first formal statement in favor of "a very slow, a very methodical, very careful withdrawal" of ground (not air) forces from South Korea, although he never said or implied he would withdraw America's commitment from South Korea.

They were especially disturbed to learn, in 1977, that President Carter had begun a partial withdrawal of American ground forces from Korea. Although Carter had to reverse his policy because of congressional, Japanese, and South Korean opposition, and intelligence reports about the superiority of North Korean ground forces over those of South Korea, and although the new president, Ronald Reagan, made it clear that American commitment to the security of South Korea is total, South Koreans are well aware that another Carter may some day occupy the White House and again cause uncertainty about their security vis-à-vis the North Korean Communists.

Another significant issue between the United States and Korea is the unification of the two Koreas, or the cross-recognition of the two Koreas by the interested powers—in the way that the two Germanies have been recognized by each other as well as by the international community. Despite the 1953 American pledge to "consult further regarding the attainment of a united, free, and independent Korea," the United States has been committed to maintenance of the status quo and to the policy of cross-recognition of the two Koreas by the interested powers. So long as North Korea would not attack South Korea, the division into two hostile camps would hurt neither the United States nor Japan, nor the Soviet Union nor the People's Republic of China. In fact, the division has prevented any power's domination of the whole and has minimized international friction over the two Koreas. However, hostilities and border incidents between the two Koreas have not only continued but have become intensified. Thus, as time goes on, a peaceful reunification of Korea seems less and less likely.

In the next chapter, Kwak and Patterson discuss the American role in maintaining the security of South Korea vis-à-vis North Korea and in positioning itself on the issue of reunification.

6

The Security
Relationship between
Korea and the United States,
1960–1984

Tae-Hwan Kwak and Wayne Patterson

As Professor Oliver argued in the preceding essay, American policy in the immediate postwar period was faulty because it did not view the Korean situation in a realistic manner. As a result, it took the Korean War (1950–53) to awaken the United States to the dangerous situation on the Korean peninsula. Following the war, the Mutual Defense Treaty between the United States and the Republic of Korea (South Korea) was signed (in 1954) to prevent the recurrence of war. Article 3 of that pact reads:

> Each party recognizes that an armed attack in the Pacific area on either of the parties in territories now under their respective administrative control, or hereafter recognized by one of the parties as lawfully brought under the administrative control of the other, would be dangerous to its own peace and safety and declares that it would act to meet the common danger in accordance with its constitutional processes.[1]

Despite the fact that American ground and air troops were stationed in Korea, the South Korean government sought reassurances that the United States would defend South Korea should a new war occur. From the standpoint of Seoul, the

existing defense treaty was an insufficient American commitment because it did not provide a NATO-type guarantee of
automatic American commitment to South Korea but simply
prescribed that the U.S. government "would act to meet the
common danger in accordance with its constitutional pro-
cesses." In other words, the United States would decide what
measures to take on the basis of perceived national interests, in
consultation with the Congress, should another war occur in
Korea.

Because of this concern, the U.S. government has frequently
felt the need to reaffirm its determination to use American
ground troops to defend South Korea, and has done so through
joint U.S.-ROK communiqués.[2] South Korea was worried because in the latter half of the 1960s the United States reas-
sessed its security interests in the world, primarily because of
what has been called the "Vietnam syndrome"—an attitude
formed by the protracted and frustrating war in Vietnam and by
American domestic difficulties, including inflation, a balance-of-
payments deficit, embittered public opinion, and a hostile Congress. In 1969 this feeling became apparent on an official level
when President Nixon expressed his desire to reduce the U.S.
military presence in Asia and to reassess American policy toward Asian countries so as to avoid future Vietnams. Nixon
stated that future American policy in Asia would seek to avoid
military intervention that could involve the United States in this
type of situation. Moreover, he restated the concept of self-help
and self-reliance when he met President Park Chung-hee in San
Francisco in August 1969. While Nixon reaffirmed the U.S. treaty commitment to defend South Korea against the North
Koreans, he warned that "all the aid in the world will not help
the people who are unable or unwilling to help themselves."[3]

This "Nixon Doctrine" was implemented in U.S.-South
Korean security relations in the early 1970s, with the removal of
some 24,000 troops by the end of 1973. Although the reduction

of American forces was appropriate in view of U.S. domestic difficulties, the United States kept its commitment to the security of South Korea by increasing military assistance.[4] Washington again declared that, in the event of armed aggression, the United States would defend South Korea.[5] South Korean leaders, however, concluded that American policy would be flexible, according to changes in the international as well as the American domestic political environments, as far as involvement of U.S. ground troops in a renewed conflict was concerned.[6]

Events in the spring of 1975, including the debacle in Vietnam and Kim Il-sung's sudden visits to China and other socialist countries, shocked South Korea's leaders, who perceived these events as aggressive. The Ford administration warned Kim not to ignore American determination to repel an invasion from the North because of American disengagement from Indochina. This warning was the beginning of tough talk from the United States about Korean security—a trend that was repeated when the issue of nuclear weapons and Korea became intertwined.

In the spring of 1975, former Secretary of State James Schlesinger stated that if South Korea were invaded by the North, "it is necessary to go for the heart of the opponent's power; destroy his military forces rather than simply being involved endlessly in ancillary military operations."[7] He also expressed the possibility of using tactical nuclear weapons in Korea in the event of a North Korean attack, stating that "the U.S. cannot foreclose any option to use nuclear weapons or introduce more ground troops."[8]

A second issue involving Korea and nuclear weapons arose when President Park stated, in June 1975, that "South Korea would and could develop its own nuclear weapons if the U.S. nuclear umbrella is withdrawn."[9] However, on January 29, 1977, Park declared that South Korea would not develop nuclear arms.[10] The U.S. government had been critical of French and Canadian sales of nuclear technology to South Korea because the United States did not want South Korea to become a nuclear power.[11] Its acquisition of nuclear weapons could trigger a new arms race between the two Koreas, might lead to a nuclear arming of the North, and, even more importantly, might stimulate Japanese nuclear armament, thereby destabilizing the delicate power balance in Northeast Asia.

Another issue in Korean-American security relations which dominated the 1970s was the long-range American goal of easing tension in the Korean peninsula and promoting favorable conditions for reunification. In this relationship are two factors (or stumbling blocks) that must be considered, one of which is stark reality on the Korean peninsula: two seemingly incompatible sets of values, ideologies, alliance structures, and political systems. The other factor is the constraint of the four great powers. Their conflict of interests makes it more difficult to reunify Korea, unless there are adjustments and concessions.

Since the United States will not allow the unification of Korea by military means, it has supported a political dialogue that would achieve the desired result peacefully. To that end, the United States supported the "inter-Korean dialogue" which began in 1971, although this effort ended unsuccessfully a year later. Since that time the United States has suggested international conferences among the interested parties, which would include not only the two Koreas but also the four major powers involved. The United States has set two preconditions for such a conference. The first is that the security treaty between Korea and the United States, which permits the stationing of troops there, not be on the agenda. The second is that South Korea must be included in any conference regarding its future.

Former Secretary of State Kissinger is on record on these two subjects:

> We will not acquiesce in any proposals which would exclude the
> Republic of Korea from discussions about its future. And we will
> not allow our military presence, which derives from bilateral
> agreements, to be dictated by third parties. But we are prepared
> now to transform the armistice arrangements to a permanent
> peace.

Kissinger also made it clear (in the same speech) that the
United States would be willing to talk to North Korea about the
future of Korea, provided that South Korea be present.[12]

President Ford discussed Korea when he enunciated a new
Pacific Doctrine on December 7, 1975, in which he expressed
U.S. determination to stay in Asia, as a Pacific power, in the
post-Indochina era. The fifth of the six principles of this Pacific
Doctrine dealt with Korea: "Peace in Asia depends upon a reso-
lution of Korean political conflicts, and thus, the U.S. remains
committed to peace and security on the Korean peninsula."
Ford elaborated this aspect of his policy:

> Peace in Asia depends upon a resolution of outstanding political
> conflicts. In Korea tension persists. We have close ties with the
> Republic of Korea; and we remain committed to peace and se-
> curity on the Korean peninsula, as the presence of our forces
> there attests. Responding to the heightened tension last spring,
> we reaffirmed our support of the Republic of Korea. Today, the
> United States is ready to consider constructive ways of easing
> tensions on the peninsula, but we will continue to resist any
> moves which attempt to exclude the Republic of Korea from
> discussion of its own future.[13]

Thus while the Nixon Doctrine of 1969 called for the gradual
reduction of American power and influence in Asia in the
rapidly changing international situation in the late 1960s, President Ford's Pacific Doctrine in the post-Indochina era served to
augment U.S. economic, political, and military participation as
a Pacific power and to defend its interests in the Pacific region

by maintaining a stable balance among the four great powers in the region.

Another actor in the U.S.-Korean security relationship in the 1970s was the United Nations. In 1948, in the early postwar years, the United States had turned to the United Nations to conduct Korea-wide elections to solve the impasse with the Soviet Union over Korea. In 1975 the United Nations again found itself dealing with the Korean question, when (on November 18, 1975) the 30th General Assembly adopted two conflicting resolutions. One, sponsored by the United States and twenty-seven other nations and adopted by a vote of 59–51 (with 29 abstentions), called for negotiations to find alternatives for the 1953 armistice agreement by the parties directly concerned (North and South Korea, China, and the United States), allowing dissolution of the United Nations Command by January 1976.[14]

The other resolution, sponsored by Algeria, China, the Soviet Union, and many Third World countries and adopted by a vote of 54–43 (with 42 abstentions), called for immediate dissolution of the U.N. Command, withdrawal of all foreign troops from Korea, and replacement of the armistice with a peace treaty between North Korea and the United States. North Korea contended that South Korea should not be included in negotiations for a peace agreement between P'yŏngyang and Washington to replace the armistice, since Seoul was not a party to the 1953 armistice. (Neither of these resolutions had any effect in changing the status quo in Korea.)

To the 31st session of the General Assembly (September 30, 1976), Secretary Kissinger again proposed a conference to discuss ways of adapting the armistice to new conditions and replacing it with permanent arrangements. He proposed a three-phase approach, whose first phase would be talks between North and South Korea to discuss venue and the scope of subsequent conferences. In this phase the United States and

China could participate as "observers or in an advisory role." The second phase would be an international conference of the United States, China, and North and South Korea, if the first phase proved fruitful. The third phase would be "a wider conference in which other countries could associate themselves with arrangements that guarantee a durable peace on the peninsula."[15] Kissinger reiterated that, to reduce tensions and promote security, the United States was prepared to have the U.N. Command dissolved as long as the armistice was preserved by more durable arrangements at international conferences. P'yŏngyang, however, refused to accept an international conference and, instead, reiterated its insistence on a peace treaty between Washington and P'yŏngyang.

Korean-American security relations became more clouded during the Carter presidency, when his new administration began to consider partial withdrawal of American forces in Korea—specifically, ground troops. The original objective of U.S. forces in Korea had been to deter a North Korean attack and to prevent Chinese and/or Soviet military intervention in Korea. By defending the security of South Korea and preventing a renewed war in the peninsula, the presence of U.S. forces provided peace and stability in Northeast Asia and protected American interests in Japan and the western Pacific.[16]

The military justification for the continued presence of U.S. ground troops in Korea began to be questioned in view of the changing policies of China and the Soviet Union toward the United States, Japan, and Korea. China and the Soviet Union sought stability in the peninsula and were seen as unlikely to promote a war. Moreover, South Korean ground troops were believed to be able to defend against a North Korean attack, although South Korean airpower remained relatively inferior. Thus the military role of the United States was to redress the imbalance in airpower between the two Koreas, so that the military justification for American ground troops appeared ten-

uous.[17] However, the American ground presence was also political and psychological, because it symbolized American determination to keep its defense commitments to South Korea and
Japan.

Even before the fall of Saigon in April 1975, there had been a
debate in the United States over reduction and withdrawal of
U.S. forces in Korea. It had been argued by some members of
Congress and witnesses at congressional hearings that the
United States should reduce its level of troops, and even withdraw its commitment to Korea, because of budgetary con-
straints and deteriorating South Korean domestic politics.

Those who argued for disengagement, without conditions,
pointed out four major reasons, which can be summarized as
follows.[18] First, South and North Korea had agreed to three
basic principles for reunification: (1) independent solution of
the Korean problem—independent, that is, of outside interference; (2) a peaceful approach to the problem; and (3) seeking greater national unity by transcending differences in ideology, ideas, and social systems. It was argued that the United
States should not interfere in Korea, since U.S. forces were a
form of external interference. Thus the United States should
leave the two Koreas to determine the future of their own affairs by themselves.

Second, it was argued that the withdrawal of U.S. forces
would be unlikely to invite a new war in Korea. And even if war
occurred, Soviet or Chinese military intervention appeared extremely remote because of two factors. If war occurred in
Korea, the Soviet Union and China would be compelled to as-
sess its impact on their relations with Washington and Tokyo,
because their intervention in Korea could bring them into a
nuclear confrontation with the United States and Japan. Also,
given the Sino-Soviet conflict, Korea was of great concern to
Moscow and Peking vis-à-vis each other. Each wanted to prevent the other from gaining a dominant position in North Korea,

and each would be deterred from military intervention in a new war by fear of provoking its rival. Moreover, if a larger Sino-Soviet conflict spilled over into Korea, U.S. forces in Korea would be in an extremely dangerous position. Thus the United States should withdraw from Korea to avoid a nuclear confrontation with great powers.

Third, American disengagement would not threaten the balance of power in Asia (although China publicly urged America's withdrawal from Korea). In addition, it was unlikely that U.S. disengagement would stimulate promilitarist feeling for the rearmament of Japan. In Japanese eyes, an even-handed approach toward both Koreas is necessary in promoting closer Tokyo-Peking ties, which are far more important to Japan.

Fourth, the South Korean regime had become more repressive in recent years; thus the United States should no longer support the authoritarian government in Seoul. Unless there was development of a free democratic society in South Korea, the United States should be prepared to withdraw its forces from South Korea.

In addition to these arguments in the United States, North Korea has insisted upon the withdrawal of American troops from South Korea, charging the United States with "plotting to perpetuate the division of Korea and hamper her reunification."[19] Kim's attack on U.S. forces in Korea strengthens North Korea's international position as a nationalist leader in many countries of the Third World. U.S. forces in Korea thus become a political target for Kim at the United Nations and other international fora.

In a press conference in his Georgia home on December 21, 1976, President-elect Carter made the first formal remarks on troop withdrawal from Korea after his election: "My stance on the Korean withdrawal will be a very slow, a very methodical, a very careful withdrawal of the ground forces after consultation with South Korea and Japan is carried out."[20] Almost immediately, opposition to this change in policy arose. South Korean leaders feared that withdrawal would increase the danger of war by the unpredictable Kim Il-sung and would cause China and the Soviet Union to perceive less cost and risk in supporting Kim. The Japanese government also opposed the withdrawal, for security reasons. Tokyo supported the presence of U.S. ground forces in Korea for reasons of stability in the peninsula, which in turn contributed to peace and security in Northeast Asia. The Japanese government also believed that the U.S. military presence promoted conditions for Japanese trade and investment in South Korea by diminishing the risk of war in Korea. Finally, the presence of American forces provided for the coordination of U.S. and Japanese policies toward South Korea and, furthermore, strengthened the credibility of the U.S. commitment to the defense of Japan.

In addition to opposition from South Korea and Japan, President Carter encountered resistance at home, notably from conservatives and the "defense community." Others criticized withdrawal because it was unilateral—that is, no concessions had been wrested from North Korea as a *quid pro quo.*

Despite this opposition at home and abroad, the Carter administration held to its policy to withdraw all American ground troops from Korea. As stated earlier, the administration felt that North and South Korea had achieved military balance in ground forces and that the air superiority of North Korea would continue to be offset by American airpower. Nonetheless, the United States attempted to reassure a nervous South Korea by establishing (in November 1978) a Combined Forces Command to increase the joint readiness of American and Korean forces. The United States also renewed its commitment to modernize the Korean armed forces.[21]

In early 1979, the situation was drastically altered. Intelligence studies indicated that North Korean ground forces were considerably larger, by about 200,000, than had previously been estimated. As a result, President Carter announced, in February 1979, that further withdrawal of ground troops would be suspended, and this suspension was made permanent in a statement issued on July 20. In that statement, it was indicated that the issue of withdrawal would not be raised again until 1981 and that restoration of the military balance and reduced tension on the peninsula would be the primary factors in further discussion of withdrawal. President Carter stated:

> Over time we will continue to adjust the detailed features of our contribution to the security of the Republic of Korea to reflect growing R.O.K. economic and military strength and changes in the international situation. At present, however, these modifications in our withdrawal plans will best assure the maintenance of our security commitment, preserve an adequate deterrent, nurture the resumption of a serious North-South dialogue, and stabilize a favorable U.S. strategic position in East Asia.[22]

Thus a major irritant in Korean-American relations was removed, which set the stage for a Carter-Park meeting in Seoul in July 1979. That the United States placed a high premium on the reduction of tensions in the peninsula and on the importance of a continuing dialogue between the two Koreas was demonstrated when President Carter, at the conclusion of his meeting with President Park, proposed direct talks among North Korea, South Korea, and the United States—a proposal that was rejected by North Korea. Since 1975, North Korea had proposed direct bilateral talks with the United States, but these offers had always been rebuffed on the grounds that South Korea was not invited. Thus the United States reaffirmed its position that it will meet with North Korea only if South Korea is treated as an equal partner. Moreover, South Korea was reassured that the United States would not go behind its back and negotiate separately with North Korea. It also reassured Japan, because such talks could be convened only after consultation with Japan, which had expressed uneasiness with the earlier troop-withdrawal program.

The Korean-American relationship was threatened October 26, 1979, by the assassination of President Park, but the commitment of the United States to the security of South Korea remained firm and was demonstrated by tangible moves. The United States issued a statement of support for the South Korean government and warned North Korea against taking advantage of the unsettled situation. Washington then sent a carrier battle group and early-warning aircraft to monitor North Korean activities, which remained within normal limits. In December of that year, when a military coup bypassed the military chain of command and reassigned troops without the knowledge of the American commander, there was concern in Washington. Martial law was imposed in South Korea, and the prospect of military rule was unsettling to the United States.

In addition, other issues impinged upon the U.S.-South Korean security relationship in the late 1970s. That negative Korean attitudes toward the proposed withdrawal of American troops were not the only source of friction in the security relationship was made evident in a series of events that came to be labeled "Koreagate."[23] Congressional support has always been crucial for maintenance of an American deterrent in Korea, as well as for continued aid to modernize the Korean armed forces. Illegal approaches to Congress by agents of the Korean government, to bolster support on Capitol Hill for a strong American posture in Korea, backfired and caused severe strain in both the alliance and the perception of Korea among the American people. By late 1978 the assistant secretary of state for East Asian and Pacific affairs, Richard Holbrooke, was able to say about Koreagate: "It will take time to overcome the damage, but we believe that the issue is no longer threatening the very fabric of our alliance."[24]

Another irritant in the Korean-American relationship (which

did *not* diminish) was the human rights issue. A yardstick in the foreign policy of the Carter administration, human rights was never intended to supersede the security concerns that the United States maintained in Korea; however, the Carter administration wanted an improvement in human rights in Korea because (1) it would ease the strain on the alliance and (2) a country that does not suppress dissent is internally stronger, more democratic, and therefore more secure. Thus the lack of improvement in human rights continued to be an irritant in the relationship toward the end of the decade. Holbrooke commented:

> We continue . . . to have legitimate concerns about practices that are incompatible with a generally free society and with close and friendly ties between our nations. . . . [Observance of human rights will mean that South Korea] can thus be strengthened as a nation, and [is] important for the healthy and close cooperation which should exist between us.[25]

In an annual assessment of human rights in Korea, the State Department reported that "after some improvement in the earlier part of the year, the observance of civil and political rights in 1980 was marked by deterioration."[26] The most serious incident of instability and, thus, of a weakened security posture was the Kwangju Uprising in May 1980, which cost hundreds of lives. The heavy-handedness of the suppression and tacit American approval may have marked a turning point in public support within Korea for American security assistance. For the first time, many Koreans expressed outrage at the American government for supporting a government that had brutally suppressed its own citizens. The Park regime, for all its faults and shortcomings in human rights, had never fired upon its citizens, and the last Korean administration that had—that of Syngman Rhee —was overthrown. Besides this incident, which besmirched the image of the United States in Korea and the new regime of

Chun Doo Hwan (Chŏn Tu-hwan), the leading opposition figure, Kim Dae-jung (Kim Tae-chung), was rearrested and sentenced to death, on charges that the State Department labeled "far-fetched."

Thus human rights during the latter part of the 1970s remained an irritant; unlike Koreagate and the troop-withdrawal policy, it had not faded away. Indeed, while the Carter administration had publicly proclaimed that there would be no "linkage" between the issues of human rights and military aid, it reminded Korea that the governmental structure of the United States required congressional approval of aid to Korea, including military aid, and that a poor Korean image would endanger passage of aid enactments vital to its security. Moreover, the human-rights policies of Korea were often castigated by the Bureau of Humanitarian Affairs in the State Department. Finally, on several occasions the Carter administration abstained from voting in international financial institutions on loans to Korea. All of these actions were indicators that—despite the words of the Carter administration that it fully supported the security of South Korea—its support was, at best, lukewarm.[27]

A final problem complicating the security relationship concerned Korea's faltering economy. During the 1970s, Korea's export-led, expanding economy could afford to spend ever increasing amounts on its defense, in addition to substantial grants from the United States.[28] In this way, the first Force Improvement Plan (1975–81) was designed to upgrade and modernize the Korean armed forces. Despite completion of this plan, however, considerable imbalance between North and South Korean military forces remained. As a result, a second Force Improvement Plan, emphasizing artillery, armor, and anti-tank weaponry (among other categories), was drawn up, to run from 1982 to 1986.[29] When this second plan was about to begin, the American government urged Korea to increase the percentage of its GNP devoted to defense to 6 percent. Korea agreed, but it was not clear that Korea's once-booming economy would be up to the challenge.

In fact, by the early 1980s it was evident that the Korean economy was suffering setbacks. The 1979 oil "shocks," high inflation, large and growing foreign debts, and a poor rice harvest resulted in a modest decline in GNP in 1980. The 30 percent inflation negated a large portion of the defense increase in the 1980 budget. In addition, inflation caused a rise in the cost of American-supplied weaponry, which placed a heavy burden on the slumping economy.[30] It remained to be seen how quickly the Korean economy would recover and be able to support heavier defense-related spending during the remainder of the decade.

In the meantime, in the United States, the fall of 1980 produced the election of the conservative Republican candidate, Ronald Reagan, which suggested continued improvement in the revivified Korean-American relationship, in contrast to the mid-1970s. The new administration stressed the need for strong security ties between the two countries; moreover, all talk of an American withdrawal in 1981 (under President Carter) was silenced. Also, it was clear that President Reagan would be more tolerant of Korea's human-rights shortcomings than the Carter administration had been.

Early in the new administration, it was evident that President Chun of Korea and President Reagan wanted to begin their relationship on friendly terms. In a significant symbolic move, Reagan invited Chun to the United States one month after his inauguration—the first foreign head of state to be received by Reagan, *before* he met with the Japanese prime minister. (Usually, new American presidents met their Japanese counterpart before they met the president of Korea.) For his part, President Chun commuted Kim Dae-jung's death sentence to life imprisonment and proposed (on January 12, 1981) an exchange of visits between himself and Kim Il-sung to renew the stalled

North-South dialogue. The good feelings that these reciprocal acts engendered were echoed in the joint communiqué released by the White House on February 2, 1981, in which President Reagan assured President Chun that the United States had no plans to withdraw ground forces from Korea and reaffirmed that the United States, as a Pacific power, would seek to ensure the peace and security of the region.[31]

Three days later, in testimony before the House Armed Services Committee, General John Wickham, commander in chief of the U.N. Command in Korea, concluded:

> For geo-strategic and economic reasons the maintenance of peace and stability on the Korean peninsula is essential to the national security interests of the United States. The threat posed by the North remains formidable and dangerous. As a consequence, the existing military imbalance on the peninsula is of prime concern and must be redressed. Concrete steps have been taken in this direction but more are required. Force improvements, both ROK and U.S., must be continued. . . . Most importantly, American forces stationed in the ROK provide the single most stabilizing influence we can provide. This presence of U.S. forces is a visible and convincing sign to our Asian friends. Economic growth and prosperity for the people of South Korea are only possible in an environment of military stability. The greatest guarantee for this is the U.S. ground soldier. His presence, with the support of the other Services, tells the world that aggression by the North will be met and will fail.[32]

Two months later, in April 1981, the 13th ROK-U.S. Security Consultative Meeting was held in San Francisco. This meeting was important because it signaled resumption of military-security consultations, which had been suspended by the Carter administration in December 1979, after the military takeover. It pointed out the threat to South Korea of the continuing military buildup of North Korea and stated that the security of Korea is pivotal to the peace and stability of Northeast Asia and, in turn,

vital to the security of the United States. The meeting also
affirmed that the United States would continue to support the
efforts of President Chun to renew the North-South dialogue.[33]

A further indication of close relations occurred in early 1983.
Secretary of State Shultz's three-day visit to Korea in February
coincided with joint U.S.-South Korean military exercises
(known as Team Spirit 83). Shultz reaffirmed the Reagan commitment to the security of Korea and visited the DMZ (Demil-
itarized Zone). Shultz also indicated to Korean leaders that the
Reagan administration was attempting to get additional funds
for military aid through a supplemental aid bill in Congress.[34]

Increasingly friendly ties were also in evidence as a result of
the Chun administration's handling of Kim Dae-jung. Reagan
had always argued that his low-profile approach to human
rights would be more productive than Carter's high-profile approach, and the Korean government, as we have noted, welcomed this change in emphasis. Reagan's emphasis appeared to
work, as President Chun, who had commuted Kim's death sentence to life imprisonment, in late 1982 allowed Kim to go to the
United States for medical treatment. Critics accused Chun of
exiling Kim, but the Reagan administration was gratified by this
turn of events, hailing it as an example of "moves in the direc-
tion of liberalization."[35]

Two events in the fall of 1983 affected U.S.-South Korean
security relations, at least indirectly. One was the shooting
down of a Korean airliner that overflew Soviet territory. This
incident dramatically worsened U.S.-Soviet relations, which
were already cool, and, for Korea, suggested that cooperation
between the United States and the U.S.S.R. on a solution to the
Korean question was impossible in the short run. It also rein-
forced the belief (held by the Reagan administration) that the
Pacific Far East was a dangerous area where American force
was still necessary.

A second incident was the North Koreans' planting of a bomb

in Rangoon, Burma, meant for President Chun. Instead, it killed a score of high-ranking South Korean officials. This incident, as well as the Korean airlines incident, underscored the unrelenting hostility of North Korea toward the Chun administration in the South and reaffirmed security as the top priority of both South Korea and the United States.

It was in this climate of East-West tension that President Reagan visited South Korea in November 1983, after visiting Japan. There was the usual expression of support and the "obligatory" visit to the DMZ to symbolize that support. By early 1984 it was clear that security concerns were no longer an issue in Korean-American relations. Nonetheless, other issues remained, albeit subdued.

In human rights, for instance, the Reagan administration was embarrassed by the actions taken by Seoul for Reagan's visit—such as the house arrest of scores of dissidents to prevent them from protesting or meeting with the president. In addition, some 400 political prisoners remained jailed—to say nothing of the authoritarian rule of President Chun. Thus there is room for improvement in these areas.

Chun has promised a constitutional transfer of power when his term expires in 1988—something that has not yet been accomplished in postwar South Korea. Such a transfer would be a welcome sign of stability. If steps toward democratization and improvement of human rights are taken, these issues, though currently not major irritants, will improve even further a relationship that, by the mid-1980s, appeared to be warmer than it had been in nearly a decade—at least on an official level.

It is important, however, to examine the unofficial level. The beginning of anti-Americanism, noted in conjunction with the Kwangju Uprising of 1980, represents a long-range problem in Korean-American security relations. Opposition groups have traditionally looked to the United States as a symbol of liberal ideals, such as democracy and human rights. Yet if there is no

significant improvement in these areas, the close identification
of the American government with President Chun may serve to
augment this segment of the opposition. To be sure, many in
Korea continue to look to the United States as a model. Moreover, many Koreans, including many officials in the Chun administration, were educated in the United States. Finally, most
Koreans support the U.S. troop presence as insurance against
an invasion by the North.

If, in the long run, the actions of the Korean and the American
governments do not measure up to the expectations and ideals
of the Korean opposition, the prospect is for a growth of anti-
Americanism.[36] Such a development should be of great concern
because of its potential effect on the United States' security
interests in Northeast Asia. In recent years, support for an authoritarian government has reaped undesirable results for the
United States in Iran and Nicaragua, and if the Chun government were overthrown, a subsequent government might not be
pro-American. Such a possibility suggests that it would not be
wise for the United States to put all its eggs in one basket. In
other words, it might not be good policy for the United States to
give unqualified support to the Chun regime as long as there are
shortcomings in human rights and democratic practice.

Despite this caveat, the security relationship between Korea
and the United States in the mid-1980s appears solid. Both sides
are convinced that the relationship has prevented war for more
than three decades. And in recent years, American administrations have viewed support for Korea as a counter to fears of a
lessened commitment in Asia and worldwide. The United
States is clearly the dominant partner, but the relationship is
not as one-sided as it was in the late nineteenth century. As
Korea becomes increasingly independent, there will be the potential for strains in the relationship, which could impinge on
security aspects. At present, though, there is room for further
improvement in the relationship, and no outstanding obstacles
loom on the horizon.

Notes

Chapter 1
Duality and Dominance: A Century of Korean-American Relations
by Wayne Patterson and Hilary Conroy

1. *Foreign Ministry Memorandum on Korea-U.S. Ties* (P'yŏngyang: Ministry of Foreign Affairs, May 20, 1982).
2. For examples, see Robert T. Oliver, *Why War Came in Korea* (New York: Fordham University Press, 1950), and *Syngman Rhee: The Man behind the Myth* (New York: Dodd, Mead, 1955).

Chapter 2
Korean-American Diplomatic Relations, 1882–1905
by Yur-Bok Lee

1. For an excellent account of the circumstances under which Kojong was chosen to succeed King Ch'ŏljong in 1863 and the young monarch became the real ruler of Korea in 1873 and 1874, see Yi Sŏn-gŭn, *Han'guksa: Ch'oegŭnse-p'yŏn* [History of Korea: The Most Recent Period], (Seoul: Ŭryu munhwasa, 1964), pp. 151–63, 342–53 (hereafter cited as *HGSC*).
2. For King Kojong's unwarranted faith in the United States, see my *Establishment of a Korean Legation in the United States, 1887–1890: A Study of Conflict between Confucian World Order and Modern International Relations,* Illinois Papers in Asian Studies, vol. 3 (Urbana: Center for Asian Studies, University of Illinois, 1983); Fred Harvey Harrington, *God, Mammon, and the Japanese: Dr. Horace N. Allen and Korean-American Relations, 1884–1905* (Madison: University of Wisconsin Press, 1944); Tyler Dennett, *Americans in Eastern Asia: A Critical Study of the Policy of the United States with Reference to China, Japan, and Korea in the 19th Century* (reprint, New York: Barnes and Noble, 1963), chaps. 24, 25, 26; Robert T. Pollard, "America's Relations with Korea, 1882–1895," *Chinese Social and Political Science Review* 16 (October 1932): 425–71.

3. Robert R. Swartout, Jr., *Mandarins, Gunboats, and Power Politics: Owen Nickerson Denny and the International Rivalries in Korea*, Asian Studies at Hawaii, no. 25 (Honolulu: University Press of Hawaii, 1980), pp. 30–31.

4. Martina Deuchler, *Confucian Gentlemen and Barbarian Envoys: The Opening of Korea, 1875–1885* (Seattle and London: University of Washington Press, 1977), pp. 15–17; Key-Hiuk Kim, *The Last Phase of the East Asian World Order: Korea, Japan, and the Chinese Empire, 1860–1882* (Berkeley, Los Angeles, London: University of California Press, 1980), pp. 337–38.

5. *Ch'ing-chi Chung-Jih-Han Kuan-hsi shih-liao* [Historical Materials on Sino-Japanese-Korean Relations during the Late Ch'ing Period], 11 vols. (Taipei: Institute of Modern History, Academia Sinica, 1972), 11:366–69 (hereafter cited as *CJHK*); Song Pyŏng-gi, "Sipgu segimal ŭi yŏnmiron sosŏl: Yi Hong-chang ŭi milhamŭ chungsim ŭro" [An Introduction to the Korean Alliance with America in the Late Nineteenth Century: Centering on Yi Hung-chang's Confidential Letters], *Sahakchi* 9 (November 1975): 61–88; Pak Il-gŭn, *Mi'guk ŭi kae'guk chŏngch'aek kwa Han-Mi oegyo kwan'gye* [The American Open Door Policy and Korean-American Diplomatic Relations], (Seoul: Ilchogak, 1981), pp. 140–43, 157–66.

6. For the content of the booklet, see kuksa p'yŏnch'an wiwŏnhoe, ed., *Susinsa Kirok* [Collection of Records of Envoys], (Seoul: kuksa p'yŏnch'an wiwŏnhoe, 1950), pp. 160–71. For an analysis of the impact of the booklet on Kojong and his government, see Kim, *Last Phase*, pp. 289–300; Deuchler, *Confucian Gentlemen*, pp. 88–89, 114–20; Yi Sŏn-gŭn, "Kyŏngjin susinsa Kim Hong-jip kwa Hwang Chun-hŏn jŏ Chosŏn ch'aeknyak e kwanhan chae-kŏmt'o" [Reevaluation of Susinsa Kim Hong-jip and Hwang Chun-hŏn's "A Policy for Korea"], *Tonga nonch'ong* 1 (1963): 254–59; Kim Si-t'ae, "Hwang Chun-hŏn ŭi Chosŏn ch'aeknyak i Hanmal chŏngguk-e kkich'in yŏnghyang" [The Impact of Hwang Chun-hŏn's "A Policy for Korea" on the Korean Political Situation], *Sach'ong* 8 (November 1963): 81–87; Cho Hang-nae, "Hwang Chun-hŏn ŭi Chosŏn ch'aeknyak e taehan kŏmt'o" [Evaluation of Hwang Chun-hŏn's "A Policy for Korea"], *Taegu-dae nonmun-jip* 3 (1963): 244–46; idem, *Kaehanggi tae-il kwan'gyesa yŏn'gu* [A Study of Korean-Japanese Relations in the Opening of Korea], (Taegu: Hyŏngsŏl ch'ulp'ansa, 1973), pp. 81–102; Hō Takushu, *Meiji shoki Nis-Sen kankei no kenkyū* [A Study of Japanese-Korean-Chinese Relations during the Early Meiji Era], (Tokyo: Hanawa shobō, 1969), p. 361; Kim Yŏng-

jak, *Kan-matsu nashonarizumu no kenkyū* [A Study of Nationalism of the Late Yi Korea], (Tokyo: Tokyo University Press, 1975), pp. 95–98.

7. Chŏng Yong-sŏk, *Miguk ŭi taeHan chŏngch'aek, 1845–1980* [American Policy toward Korea, 1845–1980], (Seoul: Ilchogak, 1979), pp. 7–39.

8. Foulk to Secretary of the Navy (enc.), in Foote to Frelinghuysen, December 17, 1884, no. 128, U.S. Department of State, Despatches from U.S. Ministers to Korea, 1883–1905, file microcopies of records in National Archives, Washington, D.C., no. 134 (hereafter cited as Dip. Desp., Korea). See also George M. McCune and John A. Harrison, eds., *Korean-American Relations, Documents pertaining to the Far Eastern Diplomacy of the United States, Volume I, The Initial Period, 1883–1886* (Berkeley and Los Angeles: University of California Press, 1963), p. 105.

9. Foote to Korean King, May 20, 1883, no. 3, note, Domestic File, microcopies of records in National Archives, Washington, D.C., microcopies 40, roll 98 (hereafter cited as NA, M-40, R-98).

10. Andrew C. Nahm, "American-Korean Relations, 1866–1976: An Overview," in *The United States and Korea: American-Korean Relations, 1866–1976* (Korean Studies Series 6), ed. idem (Kalamazoo: Center for Korean Studies, Western Michigan University, 1979), pp. 11–12.

11. M. Frederick Nelson, *Korea and the Old Orders in Eastern Asia* (Baton Rouge: Louisiana State University Press, 1945; reprint ed., New York: Russell & Russell, 1967), pp. 223–43.

12. Kim, *Last Phase*, p. 253.

13. See Frelinghuysen to Senate Foreign Relations Committee, July 29, 1882, *Report Back*, 14:653, Department of State; Tyler Dennett, "American Choices in the Far East in 1882," *American Historical Review* 30 (October 1924–July 1925): 86; idem, "American 'Good Offices' in Asia," *American Journal of International Law* 16 (January 1922): 18–19.

Shufeldt insisted that the United States became the sponsor of Korean independence by concluding the treaty; see Robert W. Shufeldt, "Corea's Trouble," in *San Francisco Chronicle*, October 30, 1887, p. 2. See also Yur-Bok Lee, *Diplomatic Relations between the United States and Korea, 1866–1887* (New York: Humanities Press, 1970), pp. 52–53.

14. Hilary Conroy, *The Japanese Seizure of Korea, 1868–1910: A Study of Realism and Idealism in International Relations* (Philadelphia: University of Pennsylvania Press, 1960), pp. 66–67; Tabohashi

Kiyoshi, *Kindai Nissen kankei no kenkyū* [A Study of Modern Japanese-Korean Relations], 2 vols. (Keijō: Chōsen sōtokufu, 1940), 1:515–19 (hereafter cited as *KNK*).

15. For instance, see China, National Palace Museum, ed., *Ch'ing Kuang-hsü ch'ao Chung-Jih chiao-she shih-liao* [Documents on Sino-Japanese Relations during the Kuang-hsü Reign], 44 vols. (Peking: National Palace Museum, 1932), 10:34–35 (hereafter cited as *CSSL*). See also Frederick Foo Chien, *The Opening of Korea: A Study of Chinese Diplomacy, 1876–1885* (Hamden, Conn.: Shoe String Press, 1967), pp. 86–93. China's only legal justification for her interference in Korea was the letter Kojong sent to President Chester A. Arthur in connection with the Korean-American treaty of 1882. For the content and significance of the letter, see *CSSL*, 3:10–13, and Chien, *Opening of Korea*, pp. 85–87.

16. For instance, see my *Establishment of a Korean Legation*, pp. 1–20.

17. Bayard to Denby, February 9, 1888, no. 285, U.S. Department of State, Diplomatic Instructions of the Department of State, 1801–1906: China—file microcopies of records in the National Archives, Washington, D.C., no. 77 (hereafter cited as Dip. Inst., China).

18. Li's letter to the Tsungli Yamen, 1887.7.4 and 1887.7.26, Tsungli Yamen, *Chao-hsien tang* [Korean Archives], deposited at the Institute of Modern History, Academia Sinica, Taipei, Taiwan (hereafter cited as *CT*); *CSSL*, 10:25. See also Sin Ki-sŏk, *Hanmal oegyosa yŏn'gu* [Studies on Diplomatic History of the Late Yi Dynasty], (Seoul: Ilchogak, 1967), pp. 236–37.

19. *Ilsŏngnok* [Royal Diary of the Yi Dynasty], (Seoul: Sŏul taehakkyo ch'ulpanbu [Seoul National University Press], 1967–72), 1887.6.29; *Ku Han'guk oegyo munsŏ: Aan* [Diplomatic Documents of the Late Yi Dynasty: Russian Archives], (Seoul: Koryŏ taehakkyo Asea munje yŏn'guso [Asiatic Research Center of Korea University, comp.], 1965–70), 1:43.

20. See *CSSL*, 10:36–37; *CT*, 1887.9.10.

21. Dinsmore to Bayard, May 30, 1887, no. 23, Dip. Desp., Korea; Spencer J. Palmer, ed., *Korean-American Relations: Documents pertaining to the Far Eastern Diplomacy of the United States, Volume II, The Period of Growing Influence, 1887–1895* (Berkeley and Los Angeles: University of California Press, 1963), pp. 3–4 (hereafter cited as *KAR 2*); Payson J. Treat, "China and Korea, 1885–1894," *Political Science Quarterly* 49 (December 1934): 534.

22. Hae-jong Chun, "Sino-Korean Tributary Relations in the Ch'ing Period," in *The Chinese World Order: Traditional China's Foreign Relations*, ed. John King Fairbank (Cambridge, Mass.: Harvard University Press, 1968), pp. 98–111. It should be noted that the royal title of Kojong was elevated, from king (*wang*) to emperor (*hwangje*), in October 1897.

23. For the provisions of the treaty in both Chinese and English, see *Ku Hanmal choyak hwich'an* [Treaties of the Late Yi Dynasty], (Seoul: Kukhoe tosŏgwan, 1965), 25:294–305 (hereafter cited as *KHCH*). See also Bayard to Denby, February 9, 1888, no. 285, Dip. Inst., China.

24. See *KHCH*, 26:294–95.

25. Kim Wŏn-mo, *Kŭndae Han-Mi gyosŏpsa* [The Recent History of Korean-American Relations], (Seoul: Hongsŏnsa, 1979), pp. 145–71; Pak, *Mi'guk*, pp. 71–104; idem, *Kŭndae Han-Mi oegyosa* [The Modern Diplomatic History of America and Korea], (Seoul: Pakusa, 1968), pp. 30–157.

26. Tyler Dennett, *Roosevelt and the Russo-Japanese War* (New York: Doubleday, 1925), p. 103.

27. For instance, see Young to Frelinghuysen, December 26, 1882, no. 85, U.S. Department of State, *Papers Relating to the Foreign Relations of the United States, 1883* (Washington, D.C.: Government Printing Office, 1884), pp. 172–73 (hereafter cited as *FR*).

28. See Bayard to Foulk, August 19, 1885, no. 69, U.S. Department of State, Diplomatic Instructions of the Department of State, 1801–1906, Korea; file microcopies of records in National Archives, Washington, D.C., no. 77 (hereafter cited as Dip. Inst., Korea).

29. Henry Chung, *The Oriental Policy of the United States* (New York: Fleming H. Revell Co., 1919), p. 31; Swartout, *Mandarins*, pp. 34–35.

30. L. B. Shippe, "Thomas Francis Bayard," in *The American Secretaries of State and Their Diplomacy*, ed. Samuel F. Bemis, 10 vols. (New York: A. A. Knopf, 1927–29), 8:85.

31. Yur-Bok Lee, "American Policy toward Korea during the Sino-Japanese War of 1894–1895," *Journal of Social Sciences and Humanities* 43 (June 1976): 84–85; Jeffrey M. Dorwart, *The Pigtail War: American Involvement in the Sino-Japanese War of 1894–1895* (Amherst: University of Massachusetts Press, 1975), pp. 43–55.

32. Dorwart, *The Pigtail War*, pp. 31–34; Tateno to Mutsu, July 15, 1894, Japan, Ministry of Foreign Affairs, ed., *Nihon gaikō bunsho*

[Japanese Diplomatic Documents], 33 vols. (Tokyo: Nihon kokusai kyōkai, 1936–59), 27: pt. 2, 296 (hereafter cited as *NGB*); Mutsu Munemitsu, *Kenkenroku: A Diplomatic Record of the Sino-Japanese War, 1894–95*, ed. and trans. Gordon Mark Berger (Princeton, N.J.: Princeton University Press, and Tokyo: University of Tokyo Press, 1982), pp. 138–43, 290–91; Claude A. Buss, "Early Diplomatic and Political Ties," in *Reflections on a Century of United States–Korean Relations: Conference Papers*, Academy of Korean Studies and the Wilson Center (Lanham, N.Y., and London: University Press of America, 1983), pp. 52–53; Lee Kwang-rin (Yi Kwang-rin), "Early Relations: Conflicting Images," in ibid., pp. 71–72.

33. Allen to Hay, August 31, 1900, no. 275, Dip. Desp., Korea.

34. Dennett, "American 'Good Offices' in Asia," pp. 1–24.

35. Raymond A. Esthus, *Theodore Roosevelt and Japan* (Seattle and London: University of Washington Press, 1966), p. 101.

36. Etling E. Morrison, John M. Blum, and Alfred D. Chandler, Jr., eds., *The Letters of Theodore Roosevelt*, 8 vols. (Cambridge, Mass.: Harvard University Press, 1951–54), 2:1394.

37. Rockhill to Kennan, November 21, 1905, *George Kennan Manuscripts*, National Historical Foundation Collection, Manuscript Division, Library of Congress, Washington, D.C.; Allen to Brown, July 25, 1902, Allen to Rockhill, January 4, 1904, and Hay to Allen, November 17, 1904, *Horace N. Allen Manuscripts*, Manuscript Division, New York Public Library (hereafter cited as *Allen MSS*); Root to Lodge, February 26, 1916, Philip C. Jessup, *Elihu Root*, 2 vols. (New York: Dodd, Mead, 1938), 2:6; Rockhill to Allen, February 20, 1904, *William W. Rockhill Manuscripts*, Houghton Library, Harvard University (hereafter cited as *Rockhill MSS*); Roosevelt to Kermit Roosevelt, March 20, 1905, *Theodore Roosevelt Manuscripts*, National Historical Foundation Collection, Manuscript Division, Library of Congress, Washington, D.C.

38. Roosevelt to Hay, January 28, 1905, in Morrison et al., eds., *Letters*, 4:1112; Dennett, *Roosevelt*, p. 110.

Actually, the real causes of Roosevelt's anti-Korean and pro-Japanese policy have been debated among scholars. Pringle and Griswold argue that the balance of power, the security of the Philippines, and the utter incompetency of the Korean leadership were mainly responsible for Roosevelt's policy of realism. See Henry F. Pringle, *Theodore Roosevelt: A Biography* (New York: Harcourt, 1931), pp. 267–70, and Whitney Griswold, *The Far Eastern Policy of the United States* (New Haven and London: Yale University Press, 1938), pp. 122–25. On the other hand, Beale insists that Roosevelt decided to sacrifice Korea and American economic interests there for the sake of American business interests in China, including Manchuria. See Howard K. Beale, *Theodore Roosevelt and the Rise of America to World Power* (Baltimore: Johns Hopkins University Press, 1956), p. 281.

In any case, the incompetency of the Korean leadership might have been only a marginal reason for Roosevelt's pro-Japanese policy. Even if Korea had been strong in her own right, militarily and otherwise, Roosevelt would have undoubtedly sacrificed Korea anyway, under some other pretext or justification, unless Korea had been stronger than Japan or Russia.

39. Korean historians are, in general, critical toward the role Roosevelt played in the final demise of Korea. For instance, see Yi Sŏn-gŭn, *Han'guksa: Hyŏndae-p'yŏn* [History of Korea: Modern Period], (Seoul: Ŭryu munhwasa, 1964), pp. 911–20 (hereafter cited as *HGSH*). Some American historians are also critical toward Roosevelt's role; see Philip Low Bridgham, "American Policy toward Korean Independence, 1866–1910" (Ph.D. dissertation, Fletcher School of Law and Diplomacy, 1951), pp. 37–38; Herbert Croly, *Willard Straight* (New York: Macmillan, 1924), pp. 190–94. For justifying or defending Roosevelt's policy, see Esthus, *Roosevelt*, p. 111; Dennett, *Roosevelt*, pp. 106–15; Jessup, *Root*, 2:6; Harvey F. MacNair and Donald F. Lach, *Modern Far Eastern International Relations* (2nd ed., New York: Van Nostrand, 1955), pp. 104–5.

40. For various interpretations of this controversial agreement, see Beale, *Roosevelt*, pp. 157–58, 234–35; Griswold, *Far Eastern Policy*, pp. 125–26; Tyler Dennett, "President Roosevelt's Secret Pact with Japan," *Current History* 21 (1924): 15–21; John A. White, *The Diplomacy of the Russo-Japanese War* (Princeton: Princeton University Press, 1964), pp. 217–18; Raymond A. Esthus, "The Taft-Katsura Agreement—Reality or Myth," *Journal of Modern History* 31 (1959): 46–61; idem, *Roosevelt*, pp. 102–7; Hong Yol-yoo, "The Unwritten Part of Korean-American Diplomatic Relations," *Korean Quarterly* 5 (1963): 78; Jongsuk Chay, "The Taft-Katsura Memorandum Reconsidered," *Pacific Historical Review* 37 (1968): 321–26.

41. C. I. Eugene Kim and Han-kyo Kim, *Korea and the Politics of Imperialism, 1876–1910* (Berkeley and Los Angeles: University of California Press, 1967), pp. 121–35.

42. F. A. McKenzie, *Korea's Fight for Freedom* (New York: Fleming H. Revell Co., 1920), pp. 77–78.

43. U.S. Congress, *Congressional Record*, 66th Cong., 1st sess., vol. 58, pt. 7, 1919, p. 6611; Allen to Hay, April 14, 1904, Dip. Desp., Korea.

44. Kyung Ju Choi, "Korea: The Politics of Survival, 1894–1905" (Ph.D. dissertation, University of Pennsylvania, 1978), pp. 175–83. For the discussion of appeals, see Allen to Hay, September 30, 1904, Morgan to Root, September 30, October 19, 1905, Dip. Desp., Korea; *New York Times*, August 4 and 5, 1905; Esthus, *Roosevelt*, p. 108; Chung, *Oriental Policy*, pp. 241–45; Robert T. Oliver, *Syngman Rhee: The Man behind the Myth* (New York: Dodd, Mead, 1955), pp. 73–89; *FR*, 1905, pp. 629–30.

45. Choi, "Korea," pp. 178–83; McKenzie, *Korea's Fight*, pp. 99–101; Chong-Sik Lee, *The Politics of Korean Nationalism* (Berkeley and Los Angeles: University of California Press, 1963), p. 77.

46. Roosevelt to Root, November 25, 1905, in Morrison et al., eds., *Letters*, 5:96; Homer B. Hulbert, *Hulbert's History of Korea*, 2 vols. (Seoul: The Methodist Publishing House, 1905), Clarence N. Weems, ed. (reprint ed., New York: Hilary House, 1962), 2:46–47.

47. Min to Root, December 7, 1905, U.S. Department of State, Notes from the Korean Legation in the United States to the Department of State, 1883–1906, file microcopies of records in National Archives, Washington, D.C., no. 166; Adee, December 7, 1905, memorandum, in ibid. At about the same time, Korean Chargé d'Affaires Kim also sent a similar note to Root; see *FR*, 1905, pp. 629–30.

48. *FR*, 1905, pp. 629–30. See also *New York Times*, December 13, 1905, and *New York Daily Tribune*, December 13, 1905.

49. Donald G. Tewksbury, *Source Materials on Korean Politics and Ideology* (New York: Institute of Pacific Relations, 1950), 11:34–35.

50. Carnegie Endowment for International Peace, Division of International Law, *Korea: Treaties and Agreements* (Pamphlet 43) (Washington, D.C.: Gibson Bros., 1921), pp. 64–68.

51. For examples, see Edwin O. Reischauer, *The United States and Japan* (3rd ed., New York: Viking Press, 1965), pp. 11–20; Deborah Claire Church, "The Role of the American Diplomatic Advisors to the Japanese Foreign Ministry, 1872–1887" (Ph.D. dissertation, University of Hawaii, 1978); E. Herbert Norman, *Japan's Emergence as a Modern State* (New York: Institute of Pacific Relations, 1960).

52. For example, see Jonathan Spence, *To Change China: Western Advisors in China, 1620–1960* (New York: Little, Brown, 1969).

53. Deuchler, *Confucian Gentlemen*, pp. 99–101, 103–4.

54. Kim and Kim, *Korea*, pp. 40–41.

55. Korea, Oemubu chŏngmugak [Ministry of Foreign Affairs], *Ku Hanmal oegyo munsŏ: Mi'guk kwan'gye p'yŏn* [Diplomatic Documents of the Late Yi Dynasty: American Correspondence], (Seoul: Tonga ch'ulp'ansa, 1960), p. 89.

Shufeldt refused Kojong's offer. Because of his old age, he did not want to become involved in the complexities of Sino-Korean-American relations; see Percival Lowell to Shufeldt, January 24, 1884, and Foulk to Shufeldt, October 4, 1886, in *Robert W. Shufeldt Manuscripts*, National Historical Foundation Collection, Manuscript Division, Library of Congress, Washington, D.C. (hereafter cited as *Shufeldt MSS*); Foote to Frelinghuysen, September 3, 1884, no. 105, September 17, 1884, no. 110, Dip. Desp., Korea; Frelinghuysen to Foote, March 9, 1883, no. 3, Dip. Inst., Korea; Dennett, *Americans*, p. 478. According to Frederick C. Drake, Shufeldt gave up the idea of becoming an adviser to the Korean government for two reasons: first, he received no officially written invitation to that effect directly from Korea; and second, he wanted to enjoy a leisurely retirement. See his *The Empire of the Seas: A Biography of Rear Admiral Robert Wilson Shufeldt, USN* (Honolulu: University of Hawaii Press, 1984), pp. 319–20.

56. Foulk to Bayard, March 1, 1885, no. 149, March 13, 1885, no. 153, Dip. Desp., Korea. Meanwhile, Kojong offered the job to Foulk. American adviser O. N. Denny and Shufeldt, who was visiting Korea at that time, supported Kojong's move, but Foulk declined the royal offer, partly because of fear of being assassinated by the Chinese, who were opposed to Foulk's pro-Korean activities. See Mun Il-p'yŏng, *Han-Mi osipnyŏnsa* [A Fifty-Year History of Korean-American Relations], (Seoul: Chongwangsa, 1945), Yi Kwang-rin, ed. (reprint ed., Seoul: T'amgudang, 1975), p. 171; Foulk to Bayard, November 1, 1886, no. 15, November 23, 1886, no. 23, Dip. Desp., Korea; Foulk to Family, October 14, 1886, December 3, 1886, January 17, 1887, in *George C. Foulk Manuscripts*, Naval Historical Foundation Collections, Manuscript Division, Library of Congress, Washington, D.C. (hereafter cited as *Foulk MSS*, Library of Congress); Foulk to Shufeldt, June 10, 1887, *Shufeldt MSS;* Bernadon to Foulk, March 6, 1887, Rockhill to Foulk, February 10, 1887, *George C. Foulk Manuscripts*, New York Public Library, New York City (hereafter cited as *Foulk MSS*, New York Public Library); Dennett, *Americans*, p. 478.

Next, Kojong offered the position to Navy Lieutenant Theodore Mason; but he also declined. (See Dinsmore to Foulk, September 18, 1887, *Foulk MSS*, New York Public Library.) In 1888 Charles Chaillé-Long, secretary of the American Legion in Seoul, was offered the position, but he too turned down the offer. See Chaillé-Long to Bayard, December 31, 1888, no. 159, Dip. Desp., Korea, and Charles Chaillé-Long, *My Life on Four Continents*, 2 vols. (London: Hutchinson and Co., 1912), 2:169; *KAR* 2:169.

57. Article 1, Section 9 of the U.S. Constitution provides that "no person holding an Office of Profit or Trust under them, shall, without the Consent of Congress, accept any present, Employment, Office, or Title of any kind whatever, from any King, Prince, or foreign state."

58. See Bayard to Foulk, August 19, 1885 (conf.), no. 63, Dip. Inst., Korea; Richard P. Weinert, "The Original KAMG," *Military Review* (June 1965): 95.

59. Rockhill to Bayard, February 13, 1887, no. 63, Dip. Desp., Korea. The United States took action only after the second Korean mission (headed by Pak Chŏng-yang and assisted by Allen) arrived in Washington, D.C., in January 1888. See Horace N. Allen, *Things Korean: A Collection of Sketches and Anecdotes, Missionary and Diplomatic* (New York: Fleming H. Revell Co., 1908), p. 159.

60. Dye to General Han Kiu Sul (Han Kyu-sŏl) (enc.), in Dinsmore to Blaine, April 15, 1890, no. 233, Dip. Desp., Korea; American Council of Learned Societies, ed., *Dictionary of American Biography* (New York: Charles Scribner's Sons, 1928–36), 5:579–80; Herman M. Katz, *KMAG's Heritage: The Story of Brigadier General William McEntire Dye* (Headquarters Eighth U.S. Army, APO 96301, n.d.), p. 22; Allen, *Things Korean*, p. 159.

61. See Donald M. Bishop, "Sustaining Korean Independence in American Military Missions to Korea, 1882–1896" (M.A. thesis, Ohio State University, 1974), p. 109; *List of Staff Officers of the Confederate States Army, 1861–65* (Washington, D.C.: Government Printing Office, 1891), p. 39. Cummins is the author of "The Signal Corps in the Confederate States Army," *Southern Historical Society Papers* 16 (1882): 91–107.

62. Edmund J. Lee, *Lee of Virginia, 1842–1892* (Philadelphia: Edmund J. Lee, 1895), pp. 467, 412–56; *Army and Navy Journal* 25 (1887–88): 590; Bishop, "Sustaining," p. 109; Katz, *KMAG's Heritage*, pp. 22, 24.

63. See Nienstead's file in "Applications and Recommendations for Public Office, 1893–97," Record Group 59, National Archives, Washington, D.C.; Bishop, "Sustaining," p. 109.

64. Yi Kwang-rin, *Han'guk kaehwasa yŏn'gu* [A Study on the History of Enlightenment in Korea], (Seoul: Ilchogak, 1969), pp. 168–69, 172–

73; Young-ick Lew, "American Advisers in Korea, 1885–1894: Anatomy of Failure," in Nahm, ed., *United States*, pp. 76–77; *KAR 2*:147, 151–52. Minister Dinsmore approved of the Korean action, but Cummins and Lee did not leave Korea until March 1891, after receiving their full salaries for the three contracts. See Dinsmore to Blaine, March 24, 1890, no. 227, Dip. Desp., Korea; Bishop, "Sustaining," p. 117.

65. Yi, *Han'guk*, p. 179; Lew, "American Advisers," p. 77; "Dye's Comment on Korea and Her Neighbors," by Isabella Bird Bishop, in *Korean Repository* 5 (1898): 441.

66. During the critical period following the death of Queen Min (in October 1895) and until February 1896, when Kojong fled for his safety to the Russian legation in Seoul, Dye acted as a "bodyguard" for the monarch. See Sill to Arthur Cran, November 1, 1895, *John M. B. Sill Manuscripts* (on microfilm), 1894–97, Michigan State Historical Collections, Bentley Historical Library, University of Michigan; Isabella Bird Bishop, *Korea and Her Neighbors* (New York: Fleming H. Revell, 1898), p. 279; *Korean Repository* 2 (1895): 437.

Dye's military contract expired in May 1896, but he stayed in Korea until 1899 as a kind of unofficial manager of the government farm.

67. Mutsu Munemitsu, *Kenkenroku* [Records of Turbulence—A Diplomatic Record of the Sino-Japanese War, 1894–1895], (Tokyo: Iwanami shoten, 1967), pp. 98–99; *KAR 2*:180–81; Horace N. Allen, *Korea: Fact and Fancy* (Seoul: Methodist Publishing House, 1904), p. 185.

68. Ko Pyŏng-ik, "Mok In-dŏk ŭi hobinggwa kŭ paegyŏng" [Background of von Möllendorff's Employment], *Chindan Hakpo* 25/27 (December 1964): 227–32.

69. Lo Kye-hyŏn, *Han'guk oegyosa yŏn'gu* [Studies on Korean Diplomatic History], (Seoul: Haemunsa, 1967), pp. 251–53; George Alexander Lensen, *Balance of Intrigue: International Rivalry in Korea and Manchuria, 1884–1899*, 2 vols. (Tallahassee: University Presses of Florida, 1982), 1:31–33.

70. Yung Chung Kim, "Great Britain and Korea, 1883–1887" (Ph.D. dissertation, Indiana University, 1965), pp. 141–42; *HGSC*, pp. 797–99.

71. Swartout, *Mandarins*, pp. 148–49.

72. Lew, "American Advisors," pp. 73–74.

73. Homer B. Hulbert, "Baron von Möllendorff," *Korean Review* 1 (1901): 247.

74. For the role LeGendre played in Japan, see Conroy, *Japanese Seizure*, pp. 37–41; Ernest L. Presseisen, "Roots of Japanese Imperi-

alism: A Memorandum of General LeGendre," *Journal of Modern History* 29, no. 2 (1957): 108–11; Sandra Thompson, "Filibustering to Formosa: General Charles LeGendre and the Japanese," *Pacific Historical Review* 40, no. 4 (November 1971): 442–56; *Dictionary of American Biography*, 11:145–46.

75. Kuksa p'yŏnch'an wiwŏnhoe, ed., *Kojong sidae-sa* [History of Kojong's Reign], 6 vols. (Seoul: Kuksa p'yŏnch'an wiwŏnhoe, 1967–70), 3:1890.2.19; *CJHK*, 5:2778–80, 2793–94; Miyaje Setsurei, *Dōjidai-shi* [History of the Same Period], (Tokyo: Iwanami shoten, 1950), 3:69; Lew, "American Advisers," pp. 74–75.

76. Yi Wŏn-sun, "Hanmal Cheju-do t'ongŏ munje ilgo" [A Study of Fishery Problems in Cheju Island during the Late Yi Dynasty], *Yŏksa kyoyuk* 10 (December 1967): 162–67; Lin Ming-te, *Yüan Shih-k'ai yü Chao-hsien* [Yüan Shih-k'ai and Korea], (Taipei: The Institute of Modern History, Academia Sinica, 1970), pp. 183, 210–11, 248–49; *CJHK*, 5:2788, 2793–94; *NGB*, 24:232, 25:371, 378–79; 36:280, 294, 300. LeGendre died in Korea in 1899; see ibid., 28:478–79.

77. *Dictionary of American Biography*, 7:526; Allen, *Things Korean*, p. 228; William F. Sands, *Undiplomatic Memories* (New York: Whittlesey House, 1930), p. 49.

78. Lew, "American Advisers," p. 75. Harrington describes Greathouse as "an alcoholic Russophile"; see his *God*, p. 298. For an interesting observation on Greathouse by Yun Ch'i-ho, see his *Yun Ch'i-ho Ilgi* [Diary of Yun Ch'i-ho], 5 vols. (Seoul: Kuksa p'yŏnch'an wiwŏnhoe, 1973–75), 4:135–36.

79. William Franklin Sands, "Dictator to an Emperor," *Forum* 84, no. 3 (September 1930): 140 et seq., and "Adventures of a Dictator," ibid., 84, no. 4 (October 1930): 240 et seq.

80. William Franklin Sands, "Korea and the Korean Emperor," *Century* 69 (1905): 581, and *Undiplomatic Memories*, pp. 54–56.

81. For example, see Komura to Hayashi, November 11, 1904, *NGB*, 37: part 1, 376; Andrew C. Nahm, "Durham White Stevens and the Japanese Annexation of Korea," in his *United States*, pp. 121–22.

82. Nahm, ed., *United States*, pp. 112–31. The Korean assassin, Chang In-hwan, charged that Stevens took "money from the Coreans to help the Japanese," like a "traitor." See *San Francisco Chronicle*, March 24, 25, 1908; Koh Byong-ik (Ko Pyŏng-ik), "The Role of the Westerners Employed by the Korean Government in the Late Yi Dynasty," in *International Conference on the Problems of Modernization in Asia* (Seoul: Asiatic Research Center of Korea University, 1965), p. 253; *HGSH*, pp. 964–66.

83. Donald M. Bishop, "Policy and Personality in Early Korean-American Relations: The Case of George Clayton Foulk," in *United States*, ed. Nahm, p. 28.

84. For examples, see Mun, *Han-Mi*, pp. 165–74; Yi, *Han'guk*, pp. 150, 192–93; Lee, *Diplomatic Relations*, pp. 179–86; Pak, *Kŭndae*, pp. 396–418.

85. For a critical view of Foulk, see Charles C. Tansill, *The Foreign Policy of Thomas F. Bayard, 1885–1897* (New York: Fordham University Press, 1940), pp. 427–30, 449–52. For positive views of Foulk, see Harold J. Noble, "The United States and Sino-Korean Relations, 1885–1887," *Pacific Historical Review* 2 (1933): 292–304; idem, "Korea and Her Relations with the United States before 1895" (Ph.D. dissertation, University of California, 1931), pp. 173–313; Tyler Dennett, "Early American Policy in Korea, 1883–7: The Services of Lieutenant George C. Foulk," *Political Science Quarterly* 38 (March 1923): 82–103; Bishop, "Policy," pp. 54–55; Robert E. Reordan, "The Role of George Clayton Foulk in the United States–Korean Relations, 1884–1887" (Ph.D. dissertation, Fordham University, 1955); Bridgham, "American Policy," pp. 26–35.

86. See Spence, *To Change China*. It is interesting that even now the leadership on the mainland is divided on the issue of modernization and industrialization in China, despite the Four Modernizations program advocated and pushed by Teng Hsiao-p'ing (Deng Xiaoping) and his supporters.

87. Rockhill to Allen, February 20, 1904, *Rockhill MSS*; Allen to Rockhill, January 4, 1904, *Allen MSS;* Paul A. Varg, *Open Door Diplomat: The Life of W. W. Rockhill* (Urbana: University of Illinois Press, 1952), pp. 11–12, 86.

88. Harrington describes Sill as a weak and passive diplomat, easily dominated by his subordinate, Allen, and making no significant contributions in his own right (see his *God*, pp. 152, 171–72). However, as I have previously written, "of all the Western diplomats in Korea, Sill played the most active and conspicuous role during the crisis of 1894–1895" (see my "American Policy," p. 94). Dorwart also characterizes Sill as an active, alert, and independent minister; see Jeffrey M. Dorwart, "The Independent Minister: John M. B. Sill and the Struggle against Japanese Expansionism in Korea, 1894–1897," *Pacific Historical Review* 44 (November 1975): 496–98.

89. Croly, *Willard Straight*, pp. 187–88.

90. Allen to Stevens, November 29, 1905, *Allen MSS;* see also Andrew C. Nahm, "U.S. Policy and the Japanese Annexation of Korea," in

U.S.-Korean Relations, 1882–1982, eds. Tae-Hwan Kwak, John Chay, Soon Sung Cho, and Shannon McCune (Seoul: Institute for Far Eastern Studies, Kyungnam University Press, 1982), p. 48.

91. Son In-ju, "Han'guk kŭndae hakkyo ŭi sŏngnip kwajŏng" [History of the Development of Korea's Modern Schools], in *Yi Haenam paksa hwangap kinyŏm sahak nonch'ong* [Essays in Commemoration of the 61st Birthday of Dr. Yi Hae-nam], (Seoul: Ilchogak, 1970), p. 288; L. George Paik, *The History of Protestant Mission in Korea, 1832–1910* (2nd ed., Seoul: Yonsei University Press, 1971), pp. 82–83; Lee, *Diplomatic Relations*, pp. 115–16; George H. Jones, "His Majesty the King of Korea," *Korean Repository* 3 (November 1896): 429–30.

92. Foulk welcomed the medical, educational, and social works that the missionaries brought to Korea, but he held strong reservations about the works of evangelical missionaries in Korea and criticized their "indiscreet impulsiveness in propagating Christian doctrines." See Foulk to Bayard, June 3, 1886, no. 308, Dip. Desp., Korea; see also Lee, *Diplomatic Relations*, p. 115; Paik, *History*, pp. 114–15; Bishop, "Policy," pp. 39–40.

93. Young-ick Lew, "The Shufeldt Treaty and Early Korea-American Interaction, 1882–1905," in *After One Hundred Years: Continuity and Change in Korean-American Relations*, ed. Sung-joo Han (Seoul: Asiatic Research Center, Korea University, 1982), pp. 26–27.

94. Jongsuk Chay, "The United States and the Closing Door in Korea: American-Korean Relations, 1894–1905," (Ph.D. dissertation, University of Michigan, 1965), p. 17.

95. McKenzie, *Korea's Fight*, p. 218; George Trumbull Ladd, *In Korea with Marquis Ito* (New York: Charles Scribner's Sons, 1908), p. 396.

96. A. W. Green, *The Epic of Korea* (Washington, D.C.: Public Affairs Press, 1950), p. 27; Spencer J. Palmer, "American Gold Mining in Korea's Unsan District," *Pacific Historical Review* 31 (November 1962): 378–91; Lew, "American Advisers," p. 66.

97. Chay, "The United States and the Closing Door in Korea," appendix A.

98. For instance, see Conroy, *Japanese Seizure*, pp. 492–507.

99. Choi, "Korea," pp. 51–52, 115–16, 189, 191.

100. For discussions of the causes of the failure of Korean reforms and modernization programs prior to 1895, see Lew, "American Advisers," pp. 79–82; Swartout, *Mandarins*, pp. 59–60; James B. Palais, *Politics and Policy in Traditional Korea* (Cambridge, Mass.: Harvard University Press, 1975), pp. 192–301; Deuchler, *Confucian Gentlemen*,

pp. 225–28. Although China had a positive influence on the Korean reforms around 1880, in general her "influence retarded Korea's development" after that period. (See ibid., pp. 92–191, 337.) For a discussion of the causes of the failure of Korean national regeneration and survival after 1895, see Choi, "Korea," pp. 186–202; Lee, *Politics*, pp. 55–85; Kim and Kim, *Korea*, pp. 103–18.

101. Nahm, "American-Korean Relations," p. 12; Bishop, "Sustaining," p. iv.

102. For favorable views on Kojong, see Dalchoong Kim, "Korea's Quest for Reform and Diplomacy in the 1880's: With Special Reference to Chinese Intervention and Control" (Ph.D. dissertation, Fletcher School of Law and Diplomacy, 1972), pp. 502–4; Deuchler, *Confucian Gentlemen*, pp. 49, 92–104, 107; Swartout, *Mandarins*, pp. 58–59. Foulk, Denny, and Jones had similarly favorable views about Kojong; see Foulk to Family, July 2, 1884, *Foulk MSS*, Library of Congress; Owen N. Denny, *China and Korea* (Shanghai: Kelly and Walsh, 1888), pp. 45–46; and Jones, "His Majesty," pp. 427–29. For some reserved but moderately positive views on Kojong, see Msgr. Count Vay de Vaya and Luskod, *Empires and Emperors of Russia, China, Korea, and Japan* (New York: E. P. Dutton, 1906), pp. 270–73; Isabella Bishop, *Korea*, pp. 252–53, 255–57; Donald Bishop, "Policy," p. 33.

103. For critical and negative views on Kojong, see James B. Palais, "Political Leadership in the Yi Dynasty," in *Political Leadership in Korea*, ed. Dae-sook Suh and Chae-jin Lee (Seattle and London: University of Washington Press, 1976), pp. 12–15; idem, *Politics*, pp. 260–61; Harrington, *God*, pp. 42–43; Tyler Dennett, "American Choices in the Far East in 1882," *American Historical Review* 30 (October 1924): 88, fn. 9; idem, *Roosevelt*, pp. 305–6; Sands, "Korea," pp. 580–82; idem, *Undiplomatic Memories*, pp. 54–55; Kim, *Last Phase*, pp. 249–98.

104. Lee states that Kojong "failed to become the center for national cohesion as did the Japanese emperor." See his *Politics*, p. 14.

Chapter 3
An American View of Korean-American Relations, 1882–1905
by Fred Harvey Harrington

1. *God, Mammon, and the Japanese: Dr. Horace N. Allen and Korean-American Relations, 1884–1905* (Madison: University of Wisconsin Press, 1944).

2. Unfortunately, many are still unpublished; see Walter F. Kuehl, *Dissertations in History, 1873–1970* (2 vols., Lexington: University Press of Kentucky, 1965–72), and Frank L. Shulman, *Doctoral Dissertations on Japan and Korea, 1969–1979* (Seattle: University of Washington Press, 1982).

3. Ernest Oppert, who tried grave robbing in Korea, was typical; he thought "kid-glove policy nowhere more out of place than in the treatment of Asiatics." *A Forbidden Land* (New York: G. P. Putnam's Sons, 1880), p. ix.

4. William L. Langer, *The Diplomacy of Imperialism, 1890–1902* (New York: Alfred A. Knopf, 1935); but see also W. J. Mommsen, *Theories of Imperialism* (New York: Random House, 1980), and David Healy, *Modern Imperialism* (Washington, D.C.: American Historical Association, 1967).

5. H. H. Bancroft, *The New Pacific* (New York: Bancroft Co., 1899), esp. p. 319. For the general subject, see Milton Plesur, *America's Outward Thrust* (DeKalb: Northern Illinois University Press, 1971); Charles S. Campbell, Jr., *The Transformation of American Foreign Relations, 1865–1900* (New York: Harper & Row, 1976); and David Healy, *U.S. Expansionism: The Imperialist Urge in the 1890's* (Madison: University of Wisconsin Press, 1970).

6. James C. Malin, *An Interpretation of Recent American History* (New York: Century, 1926).

7. Walter LaFeber, *The New Empire: An Interpretation of American Expansion, 1860–1898* (Ithaca: Cornell University Press, 1963), and the books of William Appleman Williams, esp. *The Tragedy of American Diplomacy* (Cleveland: World, 1959) and *The Roots of the Modern American Empire* (New York: Random House, 1969). A Russian view is I. Dementyev, *USA: Imperialists and Anti-Imperialists* (Moscow: Progress Publishers, 1979); a British interpretation is V. G. Kiernan, *America: The New Imperialism* (London: Zed Publishers, 1978).

8. In his *Relations of the Navy to the Commerce of the United States* (Washington, D.C., 1878).

9. Ernest N. Paolino, *The Foundations of the American Empire: William Henry Seward and U.S. Foreign Policy* (Ithaca: Cornell University Press, 1973), p. 28 ("new theater of human activity"), and Tyler Dennett, "American Choices in the Far East in 1882," *American Historical Review* 30 (October 1924): 84–108 (John Russell Young: "brilliant future"), are examples. See also Tyler Dennett, *Americans in Eastern*

Asia (New York: Macmillan, 1922), and Thomas C. McCormick, *China Market* (Chicago: Quadrangle, 1967).

10. W. D. McIntyre, "Anglo-American Rivalry in the Pacific," *Pacific Historical Review* 29 (November 1960): 361–77; K. A. MacKirdy, "The Fear of Intervention as a Factor in British Expansion," *Pacific Historical Review* 35 (May 1966): 123–39; Charles Vevier, "The Collins Overland Line," *Pacific Historical Review* 28 (August 1959): 237–53; John H. Kemble, "The Transpacific Railroads, 1869–1915," *Pacific Historical Review* 18 (August 1949): 331–43; and esp. Norman A. Graebner, *Empire on the Pacific* (New York: Ronald, 1955). For adventurers, a subject that needs more attention, see Roy F. Nichols, *Advance Agents of American Destiny* (Philadelphia: University of Pennsylvania Press, 1956), and chap. 7 of James A. Michener and A. Grove Day, *Rascals in Paradise* (New York: Random House, 1957).

11. Charles O. Paullin, *Diplomatic Negotiations of American Naval Officers, 1778–1883* (Baltimore: Johns Hopkins University Press, 1912), p. 302.

12. Earlier dates are those of Edmund Roberts (1834) and Congressman Zadok Pratt (1845), both of whom favored "opening" Korea. Four Americans who jumped ship in 1855 were well treated in Korea. See Department of State, *A History of United States–Korean Relations, 1834–1962* (Washington, D.C.: Government Printing Office, 1962); Yong Suk Jung [Chŏng Yong-sŏk], "The Rise of American National Interest in Korea, 1845–1950" (Ph.D. dissertation, Claremont Graduate School, 1970); Eldon Griffin, *Clippers and Consuls* (Ann Arbor: Edwards Brothers, 1938), p. 85n.

13. Ching Young Choe, *The Rule of the Taewŏn'gun, 1863–1873* (Cambridge, Mass.: Harvard University Press, 1972); Key-Hiuk Kim, *The Last Phase of East Asian World Order: Korea, Japan and the Chinese Empire, 1860–1882* (Berkeley: University of California Press, 1980); In K. Hwang, *The Korean Reform Movement of the 1880s* (Cambridge, Mass.: Schenkman, 1978).

14. Thousands, according to James B. Palais, in *Politics and Policy in Traditional Korea* (Cambridge, Mass.: Harvard University Press, 1975), p. 292.

15. M. W. Oh, "The Two Visits of Reverend R. J. Thomas to Korea," *Transactions of the Royal Asiatic Society, Korea Branch* 22 (1933): 97–123, noting that Thomas was Korea's first Protestant martyr.

16. E. M. Cable, "United States–Korean Relations, 1866–1871," *Transactions of the Royal Asiatic Society, Korea Branch* 28 (1938): 1–

229; James S. Gale, "The Fate of the *General Sherman*," *Korean Repository* 2 (July 1895): 252–54; William E. Griffis, *Corea, the Hermit Nation* (New York: Charles Scribner's Sons, 1907), pp. 391–95. George M. McCune et al., *Korean-American Relations, 1883–1886*, vol. 1 (Berkeley and Los Angeles: University of California Press, 1951–63), pp. 44–50.

17. In the Korean view, there would have been "no trouble if the American vessel had not abused our people"; "the destruction . . . was brought on by themselves" (Choe, *Rule of Taewŏn'gun*, and *Papers Relating to the Foreign Relations of the United States, 1871* [Washington, D.C.: Government Printing Office, 1872], pp. 130–32). The Koreans treated shipwrecked Americans well, as they did with the *Surprise* that same year—but see F. F. Low's sneers at that example (ibid., pp. 142–48).

18. Richard W. West, Jr., *Admirals of American Empire* (Indianapolis: Bobbs Merrill, 1948), p. 100.

19. *New York Tribune*, July 17, 1871. Bell knew that the *General Sherman* was at fault: Peter Kersten, *The Naval Aristocracy* (New York: Free Press, 1972), p. 265.

20. Dennett, *Americans in Eastern Asia*, pp. 417–22, 450–57.

21. *New York Tribune*, August 15, 1871.

22. Low's revealing report is reproduced in *Foreign Relations, 1871*, pp. 142–48.

23. Actually, as an American naval expert says, the advance of the survey ships was "provocative in the extreme" (Robert E. Johnson, *Far China Station* [Annapolis: Naval Institute, 1979], p. 157). The Koreans pointed this out to the Americans after the engagement: "The barriers of defense of a country are important places"; *Foreign Relations, 1871*, pp. 132, 141.

24. *New York Tribune*, August 15, 1871.

25. Defending himself against Secretary of State Hamilton Fish's mild objections to his Korean tactics, Low insisted "chastisement" was necessary when dealing with the "cunning and sophistry" of "ignorant, conceited and exclusive" Oriental rulers; *Foreign Relations, 1872*, pp. 127–30. For the expedition, see ibid., *1871*, pp. 115–48. Low also feared an adverse reaction if the Americans did not attack.

26. Griffis, *Corea*, pp. 403–19.

27. Kersten, *Naval Aristocracy*, pp. 265, 272.

28. The "actual" body count was stated in the June 20, 1871, report, *Foreign Relations, 1871*, pp. 126–29. Also see W. W. Schley, "Our Navy

in Korea," *Harper's Weekly* 38 (August 1894): 779–83. One naval officer said the Korean loss "could not have been less than 800 killed and wounded" (*New York Times*, August 25, 1871)—doubtless an exaggeration. The Korean report to King Kojong (53 killed, 24 wounded), cited in Choe (*Rule of Taewŏn'gun*, p. 227), is ludicrously though understandably low.

29. And the "largest U.S. military operation against an oriental nation in the 19th century"; Johnson, *Far China Station*, p. 167.

30. Griffis, *Corea*, p. 419; see also Kim, *Last Phase*, and Hwang, *Korean Reform Movement.*

31. So far as a treaty was concerned, Low admitted on July 6, 1871, that "all my efforts failed." He later (January 13, 1872) felt that results were "not as mischievous as feared"; the bloodletting "has convinced the Chinese as well as their vassals that insults and injuries will not be allowed" (*Foreign Relations, 1871*, pp. 142–48; ibid., *1872*, pp. 127–30). "Unless we capture the country we can't do anything," concluded one officer, so "the 'Corean' pigeon is up!" (*New York Times*, August 25, 1871). Rodgers had decided that his "forces were insufficient to attempt to reach the capital without great risk."

32. David F. Jones, "Martial Thunder," *Pacific Historical Review* 42 (May 1973): 143–62.

33. *New York Times*, July 17, August 22, 1871; *New York Tribune*, July 17, 1871. President U. S. Grant went further in his annual message to Congress (December 1871), saying he ordered the expedition because of the "barbarous treatment of our shipwrecked sailors," though in fact there had been no mistreatment; when "treacherously attacked," Rodgers had mounted a "gallant attack and . . . punished the criminals; and having vindicated the honor of the flag" came home; *Foreign Relations, 1871*, p. vi.

34. Shufeldt's letter to Senator A. A. Sargent, written when negotiations were bogged down. Dennett, *Americans in Eastern Asia*, pp. 462–64.

35. Shufeldt's *Address Delivered before the African Colonization Society* (Washington, D.C., 1877). For Shufeldt, see Kenneth J. Hagan, *American Gunboat Diplomacy and the Old Navy, 1877–1889* (Westport, Conn.: Greenwood, 1973); William J. Blinker, "Robert W. Shufeldt and the Changing Navy" (Ph.D. dissertation, Indiana University, 1973); and esp. Frederick C. Drake, *The Empire of the Seas: A Biography of Rear Admiral Robert Wilson Shufeldt, USN* (Honolulu: University of Hawaii Press, 1984).

36. Martina Deuchler, *Confucian Gentlemen and Barbarian Envoys: The Opening of Korea, 1875–1885* (Seattle: University of Washington Press, 1977); Frederick Foo Chien, *The Opening of Korea: A Study of Chinese Diplomacy, 1876–1885* (Hamden, Conn.: Shoe String Press, 1967); Il-keun Park [Pak Il-gŭn], "China's Policy toward Korea, 1880–1884," *Journal of Social Sciences and Humanities*, no. 53 (June 1981): 45–77; Mary C. Wright, "The Adaptability of Ch'ing Diplomacy: The Case of Korea," *Journal of Asian Studies* 17 (May 1958): 363–81; John King Fairbank and Kwang-Ching Liu, *The Cambridge History of China*, vol. 11, part 2 (Late Ch'ing, 1800–1911), (Cambridge: Cambridge University Press, 1980).

37. Chien, *Opening of Korea*, p. 81.

38. Ibid., p. 74.

39. Griffis, *Corea*, p. 431. For the crackdown on dissenters, see Kim, *Last Phase*, p. 308; Adrian A. Bennett, *Missionary Journalist in China: Young J. Allen and His Magazines, 1860–1883* (Athens: University of Georgia Press, 1983), p. 189. Also see Deuchler, *Confucian Gentlemen*, pp. 90–92.

40. For the treaty, see *Treaties and Conventions Concluded by the United States of America since July 4, 1776* (Washington, D.C.: Government Printing Office, for the Department of State, 1889), pp. 213–16.

41. William R. Braisted, *The United States Navy in the Pacific, 1897–1909* (Austin: University of Texas Press, 1958), esp. p. 134; Seward W. Livermore, "American Naval Base Policy in the Far East, 1850–1914," *Pacific Historical Review* 13 (June 1944): 113–35; Richard D. Challener, *Admirals, Generals and American Foreign Policy, 1898–1914* (Princeton: Princeton University Press, 1972), pp. 66, 183–84; Jeffrey M. Dorwart, *The Office of Naval Intelligence, America's First Intelligence Agency, 1861–1918* (Annapolis: Naval Institute, 1979).

42. George W. Gilmore, *Korea from Its Capital* (Philadelphia: Presbyterian Foreign Mission Board, 1892), p. 294.

43. See, e.g., reports from Chargé Rockhill, February 5, 1887, and Minister Dinsmore, April 21, 1888, in *Korean-American Relations*, 2:205–8; L. George Paik, *The History of Protestant Missions in Korea, 1832–1910* (2nd ed., Seoul: Yonsei University Press, 1971); and my *Allen*, esp. pp. 78–80.

44. See my *Allen*, pp. 98–99, and Adee's watered-down versions in *Foreign Relations, 1887*, p. 258, and *1888*, pp. 44–45. Many American

officials were convinced that it was the West's duty to spread Christianity to "pagan" lands.

45. Griffis, *Corea*, p. 470.

46. Indispensable on Korean-American relations during the Yi Dynasty are Yur-Bok Lee, *Diplomatic Relations between the United States and Korea, 1866–1887* (New York: Humanities Press, 1970); George A. Lensen, *Balance of Intrigue: International Rivalry in Korea and Manchuria, 1884–1889*, 2 vols. (Tallahassee: University Presses of Florida, 1982); Hilary Conroy, *The Japanese Seizure of Korea, 1868–1910* (Philadelphia: University of Pennsylvania Press, 1960); C. I. Eugene Kim and Han-kyo Kim, *Korea and the Politics of Imperialism* (Berkeley: University of California Press, 1967); and see chapters by John Chay, Andrew C. Nahm, and Shannon McCune in Tae-Hwan Kwak, et al., eds., *U.S.-Korean Relations, 1882–1982* (Seoul: Kyungnam University Press, 1982).

47. M. Frederick Nelson, *Korea and the Old Orders in Eastern Asia* (Baton Rouge: Louisiana State University Press, 1945), p. 181; Jung, "Rise of American Interest in Korea." The matter was of so little importance that it was handled in Congress by a first-term Missouri representative, James N. Burnes.

48. Dispatch to Minister Foote, November 6, 1884, *Korean-American Relations*, 1:57.

49. Ibid., pp. 53–65; ibid., vol. 2, sec. 3 (and secs. 4 and 5); Kwang Hai Ro, "Power Politics in Korea, 1882–1907" (Ph.D. dissertation, University of Oklahoma, 1966); Lee, *Diplomatic Relations*, e.g., p. 109; Lensen, *Balance*, p. 527; see also pp. 39–45 (and elsewhere) in Lensen. For key advisers, see Robert Swartout, Jr., *Mandarins, Gunboats, and Power Politics: Owen Nickerson Denny and the International Rivalries in Korea* (Honolulu: University Press of Hawaii, 1980), and Rosalie von Möllendorff, *P. G. von Möllendorff: Ein Lebensbild* (Leipzig: O. Harrassowitz, 1930).

50. Assistant Secretary Edwin F. Uhl to Chargé Allen, November 21, 1893; see also Bayard's view of August 19, 1885, in *Korean-American Relations*, 1:65 and 2:181.

51. William F. Sands, *Undiplomatic Memories* (New York: Whittlesley House, 1930), pp. 117–18.

52. Young-ick Lew, "American Advisers in Korea, 1885–1894," in Andrew C. Nahm, *The United States and Korea* (Kalamazoo: Western Michigan University, 1979), pp. 64–90. For shortcomings of these ad-

visers, see also William B. Hesseltine and Hazel C. Wolf, *The Blue and Gray on the Nile* (Chicago: University of Chicago Press, 1961), for Dye, and *Korean Repository, 1895*, p. 267, and *1898*, pp. 439–42; Sands, *Memories*, p. 48 (see also his August 10, 1899, dispatch to the secretary of state, State Department Archives); Lensen, *Balance of Intrigue*, esp. pp. 527, 534; *Korean-American Relations*, 2:149–53; and my *Allen*, index ("Foreign advisers"). For advisers, *Dictionary of American Biography* (New York: Charles Scribner's Sons, 1935) and *Who Was Who in America, 1897–1942* (Chicago: A. N. Marquis, 1943).

53. Andrew C. Nahm, "Durham White Stevens and the Japanese Annexation of Korea," in Nahm, ed., *U.S. and Korea*, pp. 110–36, and see Lee and Chang-su Houchins, "The Korean Experience in America, 1903–1924," *Pacific Historical Review* 43 (November 1974): 548–75, esp. p. 556n). For Henry F. Merrill, see Henry B. Morse, *The International Relations of the Chinese Empire* (London: Longmans Green, 1910), 3:13–15. But Denny and LeGendre, appointed to support China and Japan respectively, shifted to pro-Korean stands. See Swartout, *Denny;* Lensen, *Balance of Intrigue*, p. 526; Conroy, *Japanese Seizure*, p. 389; Lee, *Diplomatic Relations*, p. 124.

54. Eight and thirteen, if one goes back to 1866. I have checked more than forty biographies of these men. There is some Korean material in Justus R. Doenecke, *The Presidencies of James A. Garfield and Chester A. Arthur* (Lawrence: University of Kansas Press, 1981), and in David M. Pletcher, *The Anxious Years: American Foreign Relations under Garfield and Arthur* (Columbia: University of Missouri Press, 1963). For the end, see Tyler Dennett, *Roosevelt and the Russo-Japanese War* (New York: Doubleday, 1928); Howard K. Beale, *Theodore Roosevelt and the Rise of America toward Power* (Baltimore: Johns Hopkins University Press, 1956); Raymond A. Esthus, *Theodore Roosevelt and Japan* (Seattle: University of Washington Press, 1966); Ernest R. May's note in *American Historical Review* (1957), pp. 57–58. For secretaries, Samuel F. Bemis, ed., *The American Secretaries of State and their Diplomacy*, vols. 7–9 (New York: Alfred A. Knopf, 1927–29)—disappointing on Korea, as are the biographies of Secretaries Hamilton Fish, Richard Olney, and John Hay. But Alfred L. P. Dennis, *Adventures in American Diplomacy, 1896–1906* (New York: E. P. Dutton, 1928) has more, mostly on Hay. Alice F. Tyler, *The Foreign Policy of James G. Blaine* (Minneapolis: University of Minnesota Press, 1927), and esp. Charles C. Tansill, *The Foreign Policy of Thomas F. Bayard* (New York: Fordham University Press, 1940), have Korean

material, as do unpublished dissertations on Blaine (Richard C. Winchester, University of Rochester, 1966), on Harrison-Blaine (Allan B. Spetter, Rutgers University, 1967), on Frelinghuysen (John W. Rollins, University of Wisconsin, 1974), on Gresham (Eugene W. Goll, Pennsylvania State University, 1974). See also Frank J. Merli and Theodore A. Wilson, *Makers of American Diplomacy* (New York: Charles Scribner's Sons, 1974), for Seward, Fish, and Blaine.

55. John A. DeNovo, "The Enigmatic Alvey A. Adee," *Prologue* 7 (Summer 1975): 69–80; Conroy, *Japanese Seizure*, p. 305; my *Allen*, pp. 246–47. Adee's notes on Korea are scattered through State Department Archives; some Adee letters are in *John Hay MSS*, Library of Congress and Brown University.

56. Paul A. Varg, *Open Door Diplomat: The Life of W. W. Rockhill* (Urbana: University of Illinois Press, 1952). Roosevelt's comment is in Allen to Rockhill, January 4, 1904, *Horace Allen MSS*, New York Public Library.

57. "Korea in Its Relations with China," *Journal of the American Oriental Society* 3 (1889): 1–33; revised and expanded in his *China's Intercourse with Korea from the XVth Century to 1895* (London: Luzac and Co., 1905—the year the United States pulled out of Korea). Rockhill also compiled two volumes of *Treaties and Conventions with or concerning China and Korea* (Washington, D.C.: Government Printing Office, 1904 and 1908).

58. Rockhill, *China's Intercourse*, pp. 45–60; much of it was outdated by time of publication.

59. See his dispatch of February 10, 1887 (State Department Archives). There is a need for more research on Rockhill's influence on the Korean policy of the United States.

60. "As far as we are concerned Corea is an independent sovereign power," Secretary Frelinghuysen wrote Minister Foote (March 17, 1883), while noting Kojong's letter advising the United States that Korea "is a dependency of China" (*Korean-American Relations*, 1:25). At least one minister, Dinsmore, seems not to have known about the "dependency" letter in 1887 (Tansill, *Bayard*, p. 443; see also Lensen, *Balance of Intrigue*, pp. 88–90). *Foreign Relations, 1888* (p. 256) *did* admit its existence. Rockhill (in his 1889 article, p. 2) said this was the "only official statement ever received by the U.S. Government as to Korea's relation to China." Korea continued to defer to China until the Sino-Japanese War (see *Notes on the Imperial Commission to Korea, 1890* [Shanghai, 1892], documents compiled by the private secretary to

the commission). China recognized the "full and complete independence and autonomy" of Korea in the 1895 Treaty of Shimonoseki; but the United States insisted that Korean independence preceded that (see Adee's memos, July 1895, State Department Archives, and Tansill, *Bayard*, p. 444n).

61. Tyler Dennett, "American 'Good Offices' in Asia," *American Journal of International Law* 16 (January 1922): 1–24.

62. *Korean-American Relations*, 1:64–65 (Bayard), 2:170 (Blaine), 2:140 (Olney), State Department Archives (Sherman), and my *Allen*, pp. 289n, 295.

63. January 11, 1896, *Foreign Relations, 1896;* Bonnie B. Oh, "John M. B. Sill," in Nahm, *United States and Korea*, p. 103.

64. Paul M. Kennedy, *The Samoan Tangle* (New York: Harper & Row, 1974); Jongsuk Chay, "The Taft-Katsura Memorandum Reconsidered," *Pacific Historical Review* 37 (August 1968): 321–26; Ralph E. Minger, *William Howard Taft and United States Foreign Policy: The Apprenticeship Years, 1900–1908* (Urbana: University of Illinois Press, 1975), pp. 143–50.

65. Tyler Dennett, "Early American Policy in Korea, 1883–7," *Political Science Quarterly* 38 (March 1923): 82–103.

66. Rockhill, quoted in Sands, *Memories*, p. 29. "It would be unjust to complain of Korean politics as lacking in excitement," commented Frederick Wells Williams in S. Wells Williams, *The History of China* (London: Sampson, Low, 1897), p. 441; and see Charles Chaillé-Long, *My Life on Four Continents*, 2 vols. (London: Hutchinson and Co., 1912), e.g., pp. 364–67.

67. Seward (1868): "Public attention sensibly continues to be focused upon the domestic questions" (Paolino, *Seward*, p. 207); Theodore Roosevelt (1905): "Our internal problems are of course more important than our relations with foreign powers" (Elting E. Morrison, John M. Blum, and Alfred D. Chandler, eds., *The Letters of Theodore Roosevelt*, 8 vols. [Cambridge, Mass.: Harvard University Press, 1951–54], 4:113). See my "Politics and Foreign Policy" in Alexander DeConde, ed., *Encyclopedia of American Foreign Policy* (New York: Scribner's, 1978), pp. 773–83, and John A. Grenville and George B. Young, *Politics, Strategy and American Diplomacy: Studies in Foreign Policy, 1873–1917* (New Haven: Yale University Press, 1967).

68. For limitations on overseas interest, see Campbell, *Transformation;* Robert L. Beisner, *From the Old to the New* (New

York: Thomas Y. Crowell, 1975); Foster R. Dulles, *Prelude to World Power* (New York: Macmillan, 1965); David M. Pletcher, "Rhetoric and Empire," *Diplomatic History* 5 (Spring 1981): 93–105; Marilyn B. Young, "American Expansion, 1870–1900," in Barton J. Bernstein, *Towards a New Past* (New York: Pantheon, 1968), pp. 176–201; William H. Becker, "American Manufacturers and Foreign Markets, 1870–1900," *Business History Review* 47 (Winter 1973): 466–81; V. G. Kiernan, *British Diplomacy in China, 1880 to 1885* (Cambridge: Cambridge University Press, 1939; reprint ed., New York: Octagon, 1970), pp. 274–78; Michael H. Hunt, "Americans in the China Market," *Business History Review* 51 (Autumn 1977): 277–307. Paul S. Holbo, in *Tarnished Empire* (Knoxville: University of Tennessee Press, 1983), suggests that Americans turned against expansion partly because of reaction against corruption, as on the Alaska Purchase.

69. In 1872 the expansionist chairman of the House Foreign Affairs Committee criticized the Low-Rodgers expedition on the ground that the fleet should have been concentrated in the Caribbean (this was partly campaign rhetoric, since he had broken with the Grant administration). See my *Fighting Politician: Major General N. P. Banks* (Philadelphia: University of Pennsylvania Press, for the American Historical Association, 1948), p. 185.

70. See comments on "semi-barbaric" "yellow-bellies," from anti-expansionists, in my "Anti-Imperialism in the United States," *Mississippi Valley Historical Review* 22 (September 1935): 211–30. Racism, of course, worked both ways; for imperialists, see James P. Shenton, "Imperialism and Racism," in D. Sheehan and H. C. Syrett, *Essays in American Historiography* (New York: Columbia University Press, 1960), pp. 230–50; Reginald Horsman, *Race and Manifest Destiny* (Cambridge, Mass.: Harvard University Press, 1981); Robin F. Weston, *Racism in U.S. Imperialism* (Columbia: University of South Carolina Press, 1972); Thomas G. Dyer, *Theodore Roosevelt and the Idea of Race* (Baton Rouge: Louisiana State University Press, 1980). There is need for more research on racism in foreign policy between 1865 and 1898.

71. On neutralization, see Robert R. Swartout, Jr., "United States Ministers to Korea, 1882–1905: The Loss of American Innocence," *Transactions of the Royal Asiatic Society, Korea Branch* 57 (1982): 41–52, and his *Denny*; Lee, *Diplomatic Relations*, p. 140; Sands, *Memories*, pp. 123, 130–31; Payson J. Treat, *Diplomatic Relations between the United States and Japan, 1853–1905*, 3 vols. (Stanford:

Stanford University Press, 1932–38), 3:129, 164–66; my *Allen*, p. 322;
Tyler Dennett, "American Choices in the Far East in 1882," *American
Historical Review* 30 (October 1924): 84–108.

72. For Nelson, *Korea and the Old Orders*, esp. p. 269, has the best
treatment.

73. Ibid., pp. 79–81; Rockhill, *China's Intercourse*, p. 3 and note;
Henry Chung, *The Case of Korea* (New York: Fleming Revell, 1921),
quoting Senator Selden P. Spencer of Missouri ("'big boy' friend . . . in
whose strength and justice . . . Korea instantly relied with confidence"); Minister Allen to State Department, September 13, 1897, State
Department Archives.

74. F. A. McKenzie, *Korea's Fight for Freedom* (New York: Fleming
H. Revell Co., 1920), pp. 77–78.

75. Minister Allen to State Department (April 14, 1904; State Department Archives): "[Kojong] inclined to give a very free and favorable
translation to Article I." No wonder, for it reads: "If other Powers deal
unjustly or oppressively with either Government, the other will exert
their good offices, on being informed of the case, to bring about an
amicable agreement, thus showing their friendly feelings."

76. Allen's reports to business and religious associates, July 1887
(my *Allen*, p. 130).

77. Allen to State Department, June 1, 1903, August 31, 1904, in ibid.,
esp. p. 326; Jongsuk Chay, "The United States and the Closing Door in
Korea," unpublished dissertation (University of Michigan, 1965).

78. The fondness and condescension show through in the writings
of both missionaries and government officials. Examples are Lieutenant George W. Woods, U.S.N., in "An American Naval Officer in 19th
Century Korea," *Journal of Social Sciences and Humanities* (Seoul),
no. 52 (December 1980): 18–30, and Willard Straight (quoted in unpublished dissertation of Helen Davidson Kahn, "The Great Game of
Empire" [Cornell University, 1968]): "a lot of sheep, footless, inane, yet
after all a people."

79. "Peculiar—not to say extraordinary—character of her Diplomatic Services"—an outside view (Kiernan, *British Diplomacy*, p.
276).

80. Sands, *Memories*, p. 29.

81. "Monotonous beyond description," according to Chaillé-Long
(*My Life*, p. 345), who had been many places, including the Congo.
Americans lived well in Korea ("life is easier in the East," said Gilmore,
a missionary; and Minister Morgan sent Secretary Straight to China to

buy polo ponies). But many American visitors and residents complained about the odors, filth and squalor, and health hazards. Quite a few became seriously ill and died in Korea or soon after leaving (Foulk, Mrs. Foote, Heard, LeGendre, Dye, Arthur Dixey).

82. *United States Chiefs of Mission, 1778–1982* (Washington, D.C.: Department of State, 1983), pp. 237–38; *Dictionary of American Biography; Who Was Who, 1897–1942; Biographical Directory of the American Congress, 1774–1927* (Washington, D.C.: Government Printing Office, 1928); Swartout, "United States Ministers to Korea"; appointment papers and correspondence, 1883–1905, State Department Archives.

The first four ministers (Foote, Parker, Dinsmore, Heard) have not yet received biographical treatment; nor has the last, Morgan. There are three articles about Sill: Oh, in Nahm, *United States and Korea*, pp. 91–109; Shirley Smith, "John M. B. Sill," in *Michigan and the Cleveland Era* (Ann Arbor: University of Michigan Press, 1948), pp. 222–47; and Jeffrey M. Dorwart, "The Independent Minister," *Pacific Historical Review* 44 (November 1975): 485–502, which is the best. Besides my book on *Allen*, there is an important article by Wayne Patterson, "Horace Allen and Korean Immigration to Hawaii," in Nahm, *United States and Korea*, pp. 137–61; and Allen himself wrote three not very revealing books. See also Bruce Cumings's remarks in Warren I. Cohen, *New Frontiers in American–East Asian Relations* (New York: Columbia University Press, 1983), pp. 239, 242. Oddly, the lower-ranking diplomats are better recorded; for the colorful George Clayton Foulk there are treatments by Tyler Dennett in the *Political Science Quarterly* 38 (1923): 82–103; by Harold J. Noble in the *Pacific Historical Review* 2 (1933): 292–304; and by Donald M. Bishop in Nahm, *United States and Korea*, pp. 27–63 (the best). For Rockhill, see Varg, *Open Door Diplomat*, and Rockhill's publications. Chaillé-Long described his *Life*, and Sands recorded his *Memories*. For Willard Straight, there is a biography by Herbert Croly (New York: Macmillan, 1924) and the unpublished Kahn dissertation. There is also an unpublished dissertation on Foulk, by Robert E. Reordan (Fordham University, 1955).

83. My *Allen*, part III; *Who Was Who, 1897–1942;* Spencer J. Palmer, "American Gold Mining in Korea's Unsan District," *Pacific Historical Review* 31 (November 1962): 379–91. This "bonanza" for Americans "brought few benefits to the Koreans," according to Lee Bae-Yong's Korean-language study, which is cited in Richard D. Burns, ed., *Guide to American Foreign Relations since 1700* (Santa Barbara: ABC-Clio,

1983), p. 474. See also Angus Hamilton, *Korea* (New York: Scribner's, 1904), p. 15, and Sands, *Memories*, pp. 202–3, as well as consular and diplomatic records in the State Department Archives.

84. Homer B. Hulbert, *The Passing of Korea* (New York: Doubleday and Page, 1906); Jung Young Lee, "The American Missionary Movement in Korea, 1882–1945," paper presented at Association for Asian Studies meeting, Chicago, April 1982.

85. Jerome Ch'en, *Yuan Shih-k'ai* (London: George Allen and Unwin, 1969), pp. 16–45; Lee, *Diplomatic Relations*; Swartout, *Denny*; my *Allen*, chaps. 12–14; Lensen, *Balance of Intrigue*, pp. 23–140; Conroy, *Japanese Seizure*, esp. pp. 185, 493. For interesting viewpoints, see *Japan-American Diplomatic Relations in the Meiji-Taisho Era* (Tokyo: Pan-Pacific Press, 1958), p. 114; Morse, *International Relations of Chinese Empire*, 3:15.

86. Hyung-chan Kim, *Letters in Exile: The Life and Times of Yun Ch'i-ho* (Atlanta: Oxford Historical Shrine Society, 1980), pp. 6–11, is an important and neglected source (Yun, who was Foote's interpreter, was a member of Kim Ok-kyun's group; Kim met Foote fourteen times just before the December 1884 *emeute*); Ch'en, *Yuan Shih-k'ai*, pp. 21–31; Lensen, *Balance of Intrigue*, pp. 23–27; Conroy, *Japanese Seizure*, pp. 114–57; Möllendorff, *Möllendorff*, pp. 72–77; Hwang, *Korean Reform Movement*; Clarence N. Weems's unpublished dissertation, "The Korean Reform and Independence Movement, 1881–1898" (Columbia University, 1954); Harold F. Cook, *Korea's 1884 Incident* (Seoul: Royal Asiatic Society, Korea Branch, 1972).

87. See, e.g., Allen to Secretary of State, April 9, 1894, State Department Archives.

88. Lensen, *Balance of Intrigue;* Conroy, *Japanese Seizure;* Kim and Kim, *Korea and Politics of Imperialism;* my *Allen*, pp. 264–82; Kim, *Letters in Exile*, pp. 22–24; two unpublished dissertations: Theodore M. Critchfield, "Queen Min's Murder" (Indiana University, 1975) and Kyung Ju Choi, "Korea: The Politics of Survival, 1894–1905" (University of Pennsylvania, 1978).

89. My *Allen*, p. 299; Lensen, *Balance of Intrigue*, pp. 575–705.

90. For the Independence Club, see Kim, *Letters in Exile*, pp. 27–43; Robert T. Oliver, *Syngman Rhee* (New York: Dodd, Mead, 1955), pp. 24–47; McKenzie, *Korea's Fight for Freedom;* files of Seoul *Independent* and *Korean Repository*, 1896–98. Three unpublished dissertations: Clarence N. Weems, "Korean Reform and Independence Movement"; Se Eung Oh, "Dr. Philip Jaisohn's Reform Movement, 1896–1898"

(American University, 1971); Vipan Chandra, "Nationalism and Popular Participation in Government in Late 19th Century Korea: The Contribution of the Independence Club (1896–1898)" (Harvard University, 1977).

91. Chay ("United States and Closing Door") has two chapters on the Roosevelt decision.

92. "There was nothing we could do except fight Japan," Elihu Root said in 1930 (Philip C. Jessup, *Elihu Root,* 2 vols. [New York: Dodd, Mead, 1938], 2:62).

93. Diary of Willard Straight, American legation secretary (November 30, 1905), in Croly, *Straight* (pp. 187–88): "They feel universally that they have been betrayed. So they have. . . . Because of our treaty they have looked upon the United States as a friend to whom they could turn. . . . They all realized that the Legations would go . . . but it came as a cruel blow that the United States should have been the first to take such a step."

Chapter 4
Relations between the Japanese Colonial Government and the American Missionary Community in Korea, 1905–1945
by Wi Jo Kang

1. Horace N. Allen, *Things Korean* (New York: Fleming H. Revell Co., 1908), pp. 255–56.

2. Herman Hagedon, *The Works of Theodore Roosevelt* (New York: Scribner, 1926), p. 406.

3. Ibid., p. 21.

4. Allen, *Things Korean,* p. 251.

5. F. A. McKenzie, *Korea's Fight for Freedom* (New York: Fleming H. Revell Co., 1920), p. 98.

6. Allen's letter to Pak Chŏng-yang, November 30, 1905, *Allen MSS,* New York Public Library.

7. "The Hour for Korea," *Foreign Missionary* 44, no. 4 (September 1885): 156.

8. Letter from Arthur J. Brown to Masanao Hanihara, dated February 16, 1912, in the Presbyterian Library, New York.

9. Ibid.

10. Commission on Relations with the Orient, Federal Council of Churches of Christ in America, *The Korean Situation: Authentic Accounts of Recent Events by Eye Witnesses* (New York: The Commission, 1919), p. 8 (hereafter referred to as *Korean Situation*).

11. Letter from Arthur J. Brown to Masanao Hanihara, dated February 16, 1912, in Presbyterian Library, New York.

12. Letter of Alfred M. Sharrocks, M.D., to Hon. M. Komatsu, director of Bureau of Foreign Affairs of the Governor-General of Chōsen, dated December 16, 1911, in Presbyterian Library, New York.

13. *Annual Report on Reforms and Progress in Chōsen*, 1912–13 (Keijō: Government General of Chōsen, 1914), p. 56 (hereafter referred to as *Annual Report on Chōsen*).

14. Special correspondent of *Japan Chronicle*, *The Korean Conspiracy Trial: Full Report of the Proceedings* (Kobe, Japan: *Japan Chronicle*, 1912), pp. 4–5 (hereafter referred to as *Japan Chronicle*). This is the most comprehensive report of the Conspiracy trial.

15. *Japan Chronicle*, p. 130.

16. William Newton Blair, *Gold in Korea* (Topeka: N. M. Ives & Sons, 1957), p. 175.

17. Letter of Missionary Samuel A. Moffett (reporting Conspiracy Case to Presbyterian Board of Foreign Missions), dated August 26, 1912, in Presbyterian Library, New York.

18. Arthur Judson Brown, *The Korean Conspiracy Case* (Northfield, Mass.: Northfield Press, 1912), p. 15.

19. "Extracts from Statement given to the Press," by the delegation of church officials, dated July 29, 1912, in Presbyterian Library, New York.

20. Brown, *The Korean Conspiracy Case*, pp. 22–23.

21. *Annual Report on Chōsen*, 1912–13, p. 200; *Annual Report on Chōsen*, 1913–14, p. 127.

22. *Annual Report on Chōsen*, 1916–17, pp. 174–75.

23. Board of Foreign Missions, Presbyterian Church in U.S.A., *Eighty-third Annual Report*, 1920, p. 193.

24. For the report of Underwood, see "First Account of Massacres and Burning of Villages," *Korean Situation*, pp. 68–72.

25. Hara Keiichiro, ed., *Hara Takashi Nikki* [Diary of Hara Takashi], 9 vols. (Tokyo: Kangen-sha, 1950), 8:216.

26. Quoted in *Korean Situation*, pp. 3–4.

27. Quoted in ibid., p. 3.

28. *Korean Situation*, no. 2, pp. 9–10.

29. Ibid., pp. 10–12.

30. *Address of Dr. Rentaro Minzuno* (n.p., 1921), Korean File, Missionary Research Library, Union Theological Seminary, New York.

31. Samuel H. Moffett, "Missionaries Contributed to Korea," in *D.R.P.: The Official Bulletin of the Democratic Republican Party* 10, no. 11 (November 1975): 19.

32. This statement was adopted in the mission meeting in February 1936 at Chinju. See "The Situation in Korea," *Mission Chronicle* 33, no. 3 (March 1939): 15.

33. *Minutes and Reports of the Chōsen Mission of the Presbyterian Church in the U.S.A.*, 1936, p. 37.

Chapter 5
Transition and Continuity in American-Korean Relations in the Postwar Period
by Robert T. Oliver

1. U.S. Department of State, *Foreign Relations of the United States, 1942* (Washington, D.C.: Government Printing Office, 1962), 1:859–81.

2. Cordell Hull, *Memoirs* (New York: Macmillan, 1948), 2:1706–96.

3. Gregory Henderson, "The United States and Korea," *Christian Science Monitor*, March 19, 1980, editorial section.

4. *Foreign Relations, 1942*, pp. 859–81. For further details, see Robert T. Oliver, *Syngman Rhee and American Involvement in Korea, 1942–1960: A Personal Narrative* (Seoul: Panmun Books, 1978), p. 9, and Robert T. Oliver, *Syngman Rhee: The Man behind the Myth* (New York: Dodd, Mead, 1955), chap. 8.

5. Oliver, *Rhee: The Man behind the Myth*, p. 176.

6. Chong-Sik Lee, *The Politics of Korean Nationalism* (Berkeley: University of California Press, 1963), p. 278.

7. Soon Sung Cho, "The Genesis of Tragedy," in Yung-hwan Jo, ed., *U.S. Foreign Policy in Asia* (Santa Barbara: ABC-Clio Press, 1978), pp. 28–29.

8. Oliver, *Rhee: The Man behind the Myth*, p. 190.

9. U.S. Department of State, *Diplomatic Papers*, 1945 (Washington, D.C.: Government Printing Office, 1955), pp. 358 et seq.

10. Wendell Wilkie, *One World* (New York: Pocket Books, 1943), pp. 44–45.

11. Robert T. Oliver, "Arthur H. Vandenberg," *Quarterly Journal of Speech* 34, no. 3 (October 1948): 317–21.

12. Oliver, *Rhee: The Man behind the Myth*, pp. 208–9.

13. George F. Kennan ["X"], "The Sources of Soviet Conduct," *Foreign Affairs* (July 1947): 566–82.

14. U.S. Department of State, *Bulletin*, October 21, 1945.

15. Lisle A. Rose, *After Yalta* (New York: Scribner, 1973), p. 155.

16. John R. Hilldring (assistant secretary of state for occupied countries) to R. T. Oliver, dated January 6, 1949, reproduced in Oliver, *Rhee and American Involvement*, pp. 95–98.

17. Robert A. Scalapino and Chong-Sik Lee, *Communism in Korea* (Berkeley: University of California Press, 1972), 1:248.

18. James A. Byrnes, *Speaking Frankly* (New York: Harper, 1947), p. 18.

19. Milovan Djilas, *Conversations with Stalin* (New York: Harcourt Brace Jovanovich, 1962), p. 114.

20. Richard D. Robinson, "Korea—Betrayal of a Nation" (unpublished manuscript, 1947), quoted in Joungwon A. Kim, *Divided Korea: The Politics of Development, 1945–1972* (Cambridge, Mass.: Harvard University East Asian Research Center, 1976), p. 37.

21. Richard E. Lauterbach, *History of the American Military Government in Korea* (Seoul: Kukche shinmun-sa, 1948), part 2, chap. 1.

22. Oliver, *Rhee and American Involvement*, p. 72.

23. Ibid., p. 63.

24. Ibid., pp. 130–31.

25. Ben Limb's letter to Syngman Rhee, dated June 18, 1947, is reproduced in full in ibid., pp. 107–11.

26. Leland A. Goodrich, *A Study of United States Policy in the United Nations* (New York: Carnegie Endowment for International Peace, 1956), p. 29.

27. William J. Barnds, *The Two Koreas in East Asian Affairs* (New York: New York University Press, 1976), p. 187.

28. U.N. Document A/C/1/230 (New York, United Nations), October 29, 1947.

29. Hak-joon Kim, *The Unification Policy of South and North Korea* (Seoul: Seoul University Press, 1963), p. 62.

30. Oliver, *Rhee and American Involvement*, p. 126.

31. The most detailed account is in Bruce Cumings, *The Origins of the Korean War: Liberation and the Emergence of Separate Regimes, 1945–1947* (Princeton: Princeton University Press, 1981).

32. Rhee's much-discussed letter is reproduced in full in Oliver, *Rhee and American Involvement*, pp. 271–73.

33. Harry S. Truman, *Memoirs* (New York: Doubleday, 1956), 2:345. On November 30, 1950, Truman further clarified his war aim: "We are fighting in Korea for our own national security and survival" (in ibid., p. 341).

34. My interpretation of the divergence of policies is in Oliver, *Rhee and American Involvement*, passim, particularly in chaps. 10–15.

35. W. D. Reeve, *The Republic of Korea: A Political and Economic Study* (London: Oxford University Press, 1963), p. 121.

36. Young-iob Chung, "U.S. Economic Aid to Korea after World War II," in Andrew C. Nahm, ed., *The United States and Korea: American-Korean Relations, 1866–1976* (Kalamazoo: Center for Korean Studies, Western Michigan University, 1979), p. 187.

Chapter 6
The Security Relationship between Korea and the
United States, 1960–1984
by Tae-Hwan Kwak and Wayne Patterson

1. U.S. Congress, Senate Subcommittee on Security Agreements and Commitments Abroad, Committee on Foreign Relations, *United States Security and Commitments Abroad: Republic of Korea*, part 6, 91st Congress, 2nd sess. (Washington, D.C.: Government Printing Office, 1970), p. 1717.

2. See joint communiqués of 1965, 1966, 1968, 1969 in ibid., pp. 1718–25. See also the newspapers *Dong-A Ilbo*, February 6, 1971, and *Korea Times*, August 28, 1975.

3. See *United States Security and Commitments Abroad*, p. 1724.

4. Total U.S. military aid between FY 1971 and FY 1977 amounted to $1,849 million. Of this amount, $843 million was for Military Assistance Program, $584 million was for Foreign Military Sales Credits, and $423 million was for TEDA (Training, Excess Defense Articles) Assistance. (See *Korea Times*, January 12, 1977.) Some of the military hardware included 18 F-4 D Phantoms, 60 Northrop F-5 E and F-5 F fighters, 12 sets of Harpoon ship-to-ship missiles, and 18 advanced F-4 E Phantoms. See *Korea Week*, October 31, 1975; see also *Korea Times*, October 22, 1975.

5. *Dong-A Ilbo,* May 23, 1974.

6. Public opinion polls indicate that the American people only weakly supported U.S. military involvement in Korea. A June 1975 Harris Poll showed that 43 percent of the American people would favor using American land, air, and naval forces if South Korea were attacked by the North; 37 percent opposed such an action; 20 percent were undecided. A Roper Poll, based on 2,000 personal interviews, conducted in July 1975, also indicated that 43 percent would favor U.S. commitment to South Korea. See *Dong-A Ilbo,* June 20, 1975; also *Korea Week,* September 17, 1975.

7. *U.S. News and World Report,* May 26, 1975.

8. *Korea Week,* June 30, 1975. According to Representative Donald V. Dellums (D.-Calif.) the United States keeps about 1,000 tactical nuclear weapons in South Korea (ibid.).

9. *Korea Times,* June 13, 1975.

10. *Korea Herald,* January 29, 1977.

11. *Washington Post,* November 6, 1975; *New York Times,* October 29, 1975.

12. For the full text, see "The Secretary of State Speech," Office of Media Services, Bureau of Public Affairs, Department of State, November 24, 1975.

13. For the full text, see "President Ford's Pacific Doctrine," Department of State news release, December 7, 1975.

14. *New York Times,* November 19, 1975; *Korea Times,* November 20, 1975.

15. For the full text, see "Toward a New Understanding of Community," secretary of state's speech before the 31st session of the U.N. General Assembly, Bureau of Public Affairs, Department of State, September 30, 1976.

16. See Ralph N. Clough, *Deterrence and Defense in Korea: The Role of U.S. Forces* (Washington, D.C.: The Brookings Institution, 1976).

17. International Institute for Strategic Studies, *The Military Balance, 1976–77* (London: The IISS, 1976).

18. Selig S. Harrison, "One Korea," *Foreign Policy* 17 (Winter 1974–75): 35–62; Edwin O. Reischauer, "Back to Normalcy," *Foreign Policy* 20 (Fall 1975): 199–208.

19. *Memorandum of the Government of the Democratic People's Republic of Korea for Independent, Peaceful Reunification of Korea* (P'yŏngyang: Ministry of Foreign Affairs, September 26, 1973).

20. *New York Times,* December 21, 1976.

21. In March 1979 the newly created Combined Forces Command conducted joint training exercises, code named TEAM SPIRIT.

22. U.S. Department of State, *Report on Korea* (Washington, D.C.: Department of State, 1979).

23. See, for example, Robert Boettcher and Gordon L. Freedman, *Gifts of Deceit: Sun Myung Moon, Tongsun Park and the Korean Scandal* (New York: Holt, Rinehart, and Winston, 1980).

24. "Korea and the United States—The Era Ahead" (address by Richard Holbrooke, assistant secretary of state for East Asian and Pacific affairs, before Far East–American Council and U.S.-Korea Economic Council, New York City, December 6, 1978) (Washington, D.C.: Department of State, 1978).

25. Ibid.

26. U.S. Department of State, *Country Reports on Human Rights Practices, Korea* (report submitted to Committee on Foreign Relations, U.S. Senate, and to Committee on Foreign Affairs, U.S. House of Representatives, February 2, 1981) (Washington, D.C.: Government Printing Office, 1981).

27. See Wayne Patterson, "Public Criticism versus Private Diplomacy in the Carter Human Rights Policy toward Korea," unpublished paper, presented at 36th Annual Meeting of the Association for Asian Studies, Washington, D.C., March 23–25, 1984.

28. See Parvez Hasan and D. C. Rao, *Korea: Policy Issues for Long-Term Development* (Baltimore and London: Johns Hopkins University Press, 1979).

29. U.S. Department of State, *Report on Korea*.

30. U.S. Embassy, Seoul, *Economic Trends Report*, January 12, 1981.

31. Joint communiqué with the White House, February 2, 1981. For an argument that the U.S.-Korean relationship remains essentially one-sided, especially in terms of security, see Han Sung-joo, "South Korea and the United States: The Alliance Survives," *Asian Survey* 20, no. 11 (November 1980): 1075–86.

32. Statement by General John A. Wickham, Jr., U.S. commander in chief, United Nations Command, before the House Armed Services Committee, February 5, 1981 (Washington, D.C.: Department of State, 1980).

33. Joint communiqué of 13th Annual R.O.K.-U.S. Security Consultative Meeting, April 30, 1981 (Washington, D.C.: Department of State, 1981).

34. *New York Times*, February 7, 1983.

35. Ibid., February 8, 1983.

36. See James R. Schiffman, "Korean Protests, Worst in Chun's Rule, Take an Anti-American Undercurrent," *Wall Street Journal,* December 8, 1983.

Bibliography

Address of Dr. Rentaro Minzuno. Korean File, Missonary Research Library, Union Theological Seminary. New York, 1921.

Allen, Horace N. *Korea: Fact and Fancy.* Seoul: Methodist Publishing House, 1904.

_____. *Things Korean: A Collection of Sketches and Anecdotes, Missionary and Diplomatic.* New York: Fleming H. Revell Co., 1908.

_____. *Allen Manuscripts.* New York Public Library, New York City.

American Council of Learned Societies. *Dictionary of American Biography.* New York: Charles Scribner's Sons, 1928–36.

Bancroft, H. H. *The New Pacific.* New York: Bancroft Co., 1899.

Barnds, William J. *The Two Koreas in East Asian Affairs.* New York: New York University Press, 1976.

Beale, Howard K. *Theodore Roosevelt and the Rise of America to World Power.* Baltimore: Johns Hopkins University Press, 1956.

Becker, William H. "American Manufacturers and Foreign Markets, 1870–1900." *Business History Review* 47 (Winter 1973): 466–81.

Beisner, Robert L. *From the Old to the New.* New York: Thomas Y. Crowell, 1975.

Bemis, Samuel F., ed., *American Secretaries of State and Their Diplomacy.* 10 vols. New York: Alfred A. Knopf, 1927–29.

Bennett, Adrian A. *Missionary Journalist in China: Young J. Allen and His Magazines, 1860–1883.* Athens: University of Georgia Press, 1983.

Biographical Directory of the American Congress. Washington, D.C.: Government Printing Office, 1928.

Bishop, Donald M. "Policy and Personality in Early Korean-American Relations: The Case of George Clayton Foulk." Andrew C. Nahm, ed. *The United States and Korea: American-Korean Relations, 1866–1976.* Kalamazoo: Center for Korean Studies, Western Michigan University, 1979.

_____. "Sustaining Korean Independence in American Military Missions to Korea, 1882–1896." M.A. thesis, Ohio State University, 1974.

Bishop, Isabella Bird. "Dye's Comment on Korea and Her Neighbors." *Korean Repository* 5 (1898): 440–42.

_____. *Korea and Her Neighbors.* New York: Fleming H. Revell, 1898. Reprint ed., Seoul: Yonsei University Press, 1970.

Blair, William Newton. *Gold in Korea.* Topeka: N. M. Ives and Sons, 1957.

Blinker, William J. "Robert W. Shufeldt and the Changing Navy." Ph.D. dissertation, Indiana University, 1973.

Board of Foreign Missions, Presbyterian Church in the U.S.A. *The Eighty-Third Annual Report.* Philadelphia: Presbyterian Foreign Mission Board, 1920.

Boettcher, Robert, and Gordon L. Freedman. *Gifts of Deceit: Sun Myung Moon, Tongsun Park and the Korean Scandal.* New York: Holt, Rinehart, and Winston, 1980.

Braisted, William R. *The United States Navy in the Pacific, 1897–1909.* Austin: University of Texas Press, 1958.

Bridgham, Philip Low. "American Policy toward Korean Independence, 1866–1910." Ph.D. dissertation, Fletcher School of Law and Diplomacy, 1951.

Brown, Arthur Judson. *The Korean Conspiracy Case.* Northfield, Mass.: Northfield Press, 1912.

Burns, Richard D., ed. *Guide to American Foreign Relations since 1700.* Santa Barbara: ABC-Clio Press, 1983.

Buss, Claude A. "Early Diplomatic and Political Ties." Academy of Korean Studies and the Wilson Center, ed. In *Reflections on a Century of United States–Korean Relations: Conference Papers.* Lanham, N.Y., and London: University Press of America, 1983.

Byrnes, James A. *Speaking Frankly.* New York: Harper, 1947.

Cable, E. M. "United States–Korean Relations, 1866–1871." *Transactions of the Royal Asiatic Society, Korea Branch* 28 (1938): 1–229.

Campbell, Charles S., Jr. *The Transformation of American Foreign Relations, 1865–1900.* New York: Harper and Row, 1976.

Carnegie Endowment for International Peace, Division of International Law. *Korea: Treaties and Agreements.* Washington, D.C.: Gibson Brothers, 1921.

Chaillé-Long, Charles. *My Life on Four Continents.* 2 vols. London: Hutchinson and Co., 1912.

Challener, Richard D. *Admirals, Generals and American Foreign Policy, 1898–1914.* Princeton: Princeton University Press, 1972.

Chandra, Vipan. "Nationalism and Popular Participation in Government in Late 19th Century Korea: The Contribution of the Independence Club (1896–1898)." Ph.D. dissertation, Harvard University, 1977.

Chay, Jongsuk. "The Taft-Katsura Memorandum Reconsidered." *Pacific Historical Review* 37 (August 1968): 321–26.

———. "The United States and the Closing Door in Korea: American-Korean Relations, 1894–1905." Ph.D. dissertation, University of Michigan, 1965.

Ch'en, Jerome. *Yuan Shih-k'ai*. London: George Allen and Unwin, 1969.

Chien, Frederick Foo. *The Opening of Korea: A Study of Chinese Diplomacy, 1876–1885*. Hamden, Conn.: Shoe String Press, 1967.

China, National Palace Museum, ed. *Ch'ing Kuang-hsü ch'ao Chung-Jih chiao-she shih-liao* [Documents on Sino-Japanese Relations during the Kuang-hsü Reign]. 44 vols. Peking: National Palace Museum, 1932.

Cho Hang-nae. "Hwang Chun-hŏn ŭi Chosŏn ch'aeknyak e Taehan kŏmt'o" [Evaluation of Hwang Chun-hŏn's "A Policy for Korea"]. *Taegu-dae nonmum-jip* 3 (1963).

———. *Kaehanggi tae-il kwan'gyesa yŏn'gu* [A Study of Korean-Japanese Relations in the Opening of Korea]. Taegu: Hyŏngsŏl ch'ulp'ansa, 1973.

Cho, Soon Sung. "The Genesis of Tragedy." Yung-hwan Jo, ed. *U.S. Foreign Policy in Asia*. Santa Barbara: ABC-Clio Press, 1978.

Choe, Ching Young. *The Rule of the Taewŏn'gun, 1863–1873*. Cambridge, Mass.: Harvard University Press, 1972.

Choi, Kyung Ju. "Korea: The Politics of Survival, 1894–1905." Ph.D. dissertation, University of Pennsylvania, 1978.

Chŏng Yong-sŏk. *Miguk ŭi taeHan chŏngch'aek, 1845–1980* [American Policy toward Korea, 1845–1980]. Seoul: Ilchogak, 1979.

——— [Jung, Yong Suk]. "The Rise of American National Interest in Korea, 1845–1950." Ph.D. dissertation, Claremont Graduate School, 1970.

Chōsen Sōtokufu. *Annual Report on Reforms and Progress in Chōsen, 1912–1913*. Keijō: Government General of Chōsen, 1914.

Chun, Hae-jong. "Sino-Korean Tributary Relations in the Ch'ing Period." John King Fairbank, ed. *The Chinese World Order: Traditional China's Foreign Relations*. Cambridge, Mass.: Harvard University Press, 1968.

Chung, Henry. *The Oriental Policy of the United States*. New York: Fleming H. Revell, 1919.

Chung, Young-iob. "U.S. Economic Aid to South Korea after World War

II." Andrew C. Nahm, ed. *The United States and Korea: American-Korean Relations, 1866–1976.* Kalamazoo: Center for Korean Studies, Western Michigan University, 1979.

Church, Deborah Claire. "The Role of the American Diplomatic Advisors to the Japanese Foreign Ministry, 1872–1887." Ph.D. dissertation, University of Hawaii, 1978.

Clough, Ralph N. *Deterrence and Defense in Korea: The Role of U.S. Forces.* Washington, D.C.: Brookings Institution, 1976.

Cohen, Warren I. *New Frontiers in American–East Asian Relations.* New York: Columbia University Press, 1983.

Commission on Relations with the Orient of the Federal Council of the Churches of Christ in America. *The Korean Situation: Authentic Accounts of Recent Events by Eye Witnesses.* New York: Commission on Relations with the Orient of the Federal Council of the Churches of Christ in America, 1919.

Conroy, Hilary. *The Japanese Seizure of Korea, 1868–1910: A Study of Realism and Idealism in International Relations.* Philadelphia: University of Pennsylvania Press, 1960.

Cook, Harold F. *Korea's 1884 Incident: Its Background and Kim Ok-kyun's Elusive Dream.* Seoul: Royal Asiatic Society, Korea Branch, 1972.

Croly, Herbert. *Willard Straight.* New York: Macmillan, 1924.

Cummins, Edmund H. "The Signal Corps in the Confederate States Army." *Southern Historical Society Papers* 16 (1882): 91–107.

DeConde, Alexander, ed. *Encyclopedia of American Foreign Policy.* New York: Scribner's, 1978.

Dementyev, I. *USA: Imperialists and Anti-Imperialists.* Moscow: Progress Publishers, 1979.

Democratic People's Republic of Korea. *Memorandum of the Government of the Democratic People's Republic of Korea for Independent, Peaceful Reunification of Korea.* P'yŏngyang, 1973.

Dennett, Tyler. "American Choices in the Far East in 1882." *American Historical Review* 30 (October 1924): 84–108.

———. "American 'Good Offices' in Asia." *American Journal of International Law* 16, no. 1 (1922): 1–24.

———. "Early American Policy in Korea, 1883–7: The Services of Lieutenant George Clayton Foulk." *Political Science Quarterly* 38 (March 1923): 82–103.

———. "President Roosevelt's Secret Pact with Japan." *Current History* 21 (1924): 598–602.

_____. *Roosevelt and the Russo-Japanese War.* New York: Doubleday, 1925.

Dennis, Alfred L. P. *Adventures in American Diplomacy, 1896–1906.* New York: Dutton, 1928.

Denny, Owen N. *China and Korea.* Shanghai: Kelly and Walsh, 1888.

DeNovo, John A. "The Enigmatic Alvey A. Adee." *Prologue* 7 (Summer 1975): 69–80.

Deuchler, Martina. *Confucian Gentlemen and Barbarian Envoys: The Opening of Korea, 1875–1885.* Seattle and London: University of Washington Press, 1977.

Djilas, Milovan. *Conversations with Stalin.* New York: Harcourt Brace Jovanovich, 1962.

Doenecke, Justus R. *The Presidencies of James A. Garfield and Chester A. Arthur.* Lawrence: University of Kansas Press, 1981.

Dong-A Ilbo

Dorwart, Jeffrey M. "The Independent Minister: John M. B. Sill and the Struggle against Japanese Expansionism in Korea, 1894–1897." *Pacific Historical Review* 44 (November 1975): 485–502.

_____. *The Office of Naval Intelligence, America's First Intelligence Agency, 1861–1918.* Annapolis: Naval Institute, 1979.

_____. *The Pigtail War: American Involvement in the Sino-Japanese War of 1894–1895.* Amherst: University of Massachusetts Press, 1975.

Drake, Frederick C. *The Empire of the Seas: A Biography of Rear Admiral Robert Wilson Shufeldt, USN.* Honolulu: University of Hawaii Press, 1984.

Dulles, Foster Rhea. *Prelude to World Power.* New York: Macmillan, 1965.

Dyer, Thomas G. *Theodore Roosevelt and the Idea of Race.* Baton Rouge: Louisiana State University Press, 1980.

Esthus, Raymond A. "The Taft-Katsura Agreement—Reality or Myth?" *Journal of Modern History* 31 (1959): 46–61.

_____. *Theodore Roosevelt and Japan.* Seattle: University of Washington Press, 1966.

Fairbank, John King, and Kwang-Ching Liu. *The Cambridge History of China.* 11:2 (Late Ch'ing, 1800–1911). Cambridge: Cambridge University Press, 1980.

Foulk, George C. *Foulk Manuscripts.* Washington, D.C., Library of Congress.

_____. *Foulk Manuscripts.* New York, New York Public Library.

Gale, James S. "The Fate of the *General Sherman.*" *Korean Repository* 2 (1895): 252–54.

Gilmore, George W. *Korea from Its Capital.* Philadelphia: Presbyterian Foreign Mission Board, 1892.

Goodrich, Leland A. *A Study of United States Policy in the United Nations.* New York: Carnegie Endowment for International Peace, 1956.

Graebner, Norman A. *Empire on the Pacific.* New York: Ronald, 1955.

Green, A. W. *The Epic of Korea.* Washington, D.C.: Public Affairs Press, 1950.

Grenville, John A., and George B. Young. *Politics, Strategy and American Diplomacy: Studies in Foreign Policy, 1873–1917.* New Haven: Yale University Press, 1967.

Griffin, Eldon. *Clippers and Consuls.* Ann Arbor: Edwards Brothers, 1938.

Griffis, William E. *Corea, the Hermit Nation.* New York: Charles Scribner's Sons, 1907.

Griswold, A. Whitney. *The Far Eastern Policy of the United States.* New Haven and London: Yale University Press, 1938.

Hagedon, Herman. *The Works of Theodore Roosevelt.* New York: Charles Scribner's Sons, 1926.

Hagan, Kenneth J. *American Gunboat Diplomacy and the Old Navy, 1877–1889.* Westport, Conn.: Greenwood Press, 1973.

Hamilton, Angus. *Korea.* New York: Scribner's, 1904.

Han Sung-joo. "South Korea and the United States: The Alliance Survives." *Asian Survey* 20, no. 11 (November 1980): 1075–86.

Hara Keiichiro, ed. *Hara Takashi nikki* [Diary of Hara Takashi]. 9 vols. Tokyo: Kangen-sha, 1950.

Harrington, Fred Harvey. "Anti-Imperialism in the United States." *Mississippi Valley Historical Review* 22 (September 1935): 211–30.

————. *Fighting Politician: Major General N. P. Banks.* Philadelphia: University of Pennsylvania Press, 1948.

————. *God, Mammon, and the Japanese: Dr. Horace N. Allen and Korean-American Relations, 1884–1905.* Madison: University of Wisconsin Press, 1944.

————. "Politics and Foreign Policy." Alexander DeConde, ed. *Encyclopedia of American Foreign Policy.* New York: Scribner, 1978.

Harrison, Selig S. "One Korea." *Foreign Policy* 17 (Winter 1974–75): 35–62.

Hasan, Parvez, and D. C. Rao. *Korea: Policy Issues for Long-Term Development.* Baltimore and London: Johns Hopkins University Press, 1979.

Healy, David. *Modern Imperialism.* Washington, D.C.: American Historical Association, 1967.

_____. *U.S. Expansionism: The Imperialist Urge in the 1890's.* Madison: University of Wisconsin Press, 1970.

Hesseltine, William B., and Hazel C. Wolf. *The Blue and Gray on the Nile.* Chicago: University of Chicago Press, 1961.

Hō Takushu. *Meiji shoki Nis-Sen kankei no kenkyū* [A Study of Japanese-Korean-Chinese Relations during the Early Meiji Era]. Tokyo: Hanawa shobō, 1969.

Holbo, Paul S. *Tarnished Empire.* Knoxville: University of Tennessee Press, 1983.

Hong Yol-yoo. "The Unwritten Part of Korean-American Diplomatic Relations." *Korean Quarterly* 5 (1963).

Horsman, Reginald. *Race and Manifest Destiny.* Cambridge, Mass.: Harvard University Press, 1981.

Houchins, Lee, and Chang-su Houchins. "The Korean Experience in America, 1903–1924." *Pacific Historical Review* 43 (November 1974): 548–75.

Hulbert, Homer B. "Baron von Möllendorff." *Korean Review* 1 (1901): 245–52.

_____. *Hulbert's History of Korea.* 2 vols., Seoul: The Methodist Publishing House, 1905; Clarence N. Weems, ed., reprint ed., New York: Hilary House, 1962.

_____. *The Passing of Korea.* New York: Doubleday and Page, 1906.

Hull, Cordell. *Memoirs.* New York: Macmillan, 1948.

Hunt, Michael H. "Americans in the China Market." *Business History Review* 51 (1977): 277–307.

Hwang, In K. *The Korean Reform Movement of the 1880s.* Cambridge, Mass.: Schenkman, 1978.

Ilsŏngnok [Royal Diary of the Yi Dynasty]. Seoul: Sŏul taehakkyo ch'ulp'anbu [Seoul National University Press], 1967–72.

Independent [Dongnip shinmun], a newspaper.

Institute of Modern History, ed. *Ch'ing-chi Chung-Jih-Han Kuan-hsi shih-liao* [Historical Materials on Sino-Japanese-Korean Relations during the Late Ch'ing Perod]. 11 vols. Taipei: Institute of Modern History, Academia Sinica, 1972.

International Institute for Strategic Studies. *The Military Balance,*

1976–1977. London: International Institute for Strategic Studies, 1976.

Japan, Ministry of Foreign Affairs, ed. *Nihon gaikō bunsho* [Japanese Diplomatic Documents]. 33 vols. Tokyo: Nihon kokusai kyōkai, 1936–59.

Japan Chronicle. The Korean Conspiracy Trial: Full Report of the Proceedings. Kobe: Office of the *Japan Chronicle,* 1912.

Jessup, Philip C. *Elihu Root.* 2 vols. New York: Dodd, Mead, 1938.

Johnson, Robert E. *Far China Station.* Annapolis: Naval Institute, 1979.

Jones, David F. "Martial Thunder." *Pacific Historical Review* 42 (May 1973): 143–62.

Jones, George H. "His Majesty the King of Korea." *Korea Repository* 3 (November 1896): 423–30.

Kahn, Helen Davidson. "The Great Game of Empire." Ph.D. dissertation, Cornell University, 1968.

Katz, Herman M. *KMAG's Heritage: The Story of Brigadier General William McEntire Dye.* Seoul: Headquarters of Eighth United States Army, n.d.

Kemble, John H. "The Transpacific Railroads, 1869–1915." *Pacific Historical Review* 18 (August 1949): 331–43.

Kennan, George F. *Kennan Manuscripts.* Washington, D.C., Library of Congress.

————— ["X"]. "The Sources of Soviet Conduct." *Foreign Affairs* (July 1947): 566–82.

Kennedy, Paul M. *The Samoan Tangle.* New York: Harper and Row, 1974.

Kersten, Peter. *The Naval Aristocracy.* New York: Free Press, 1972.

Kiernan, V. G. *British Diplomacy in China, 1880 to 1885.* Cambridge: Cambridge University Press, 1939; reprint ed., New York: Octagon, 1970.

—————. *America, the New Imperialism.* London: Zed, 1978.

Kim, C. I. Eugene, and Han-Kyo Kim. *Korea and the Politics of Imperialism, 1876–1910.* Berkeley and Los Angeles: University of California Press, 1967.

Kim, Dalchoong. "Korea's Quest for Reform and Diplomacy in the 1880's: With Special Reference to Chinese Intervention and Control." Ph.D. dissertation, Fletcher School of Law and Diplomacy, 1972.

Kim, Hak-joon. *The Unification Policy of South and North Korea.* Seoul: Seoul National University Press, 1963.

Kim, Hyung-chan. *Letters in Exile: The Life and Times of Yun Ch'i-ho.* Atlanta: Oxford Historical Shrine Society, 1980.

Kim, Joungwon A. *Divided Korea: The Politics of Development, 1945– 1972.* Cambridge, Mass.: East Asian Research Center, Harvard University, 1976.

Kim, Key-Hiuk. *The Last Phase of the East Asian World Order: Korea, Japan, and the Chinese Empire, 1860–1882.* Berkeley, Los Angeles, and London: University of California Press, 1980.

Kim Si-t'ae. "Hwang Chun-hŏn ŭi Chosŏn ch'aeknyak i Hanmal chŏngguk-e kkich'in yŏnghyang" [The Impact of Hwang Chun-hŏn's "A Policy for Korea" on the Korean Political Situation]. *Sach'ong* 8 (November 1963): 81–89.

Kim Wŏn-mo. *Kŭndae Han-Mi gyosŏpsa* [The Recent History of Korean-American Relations]. Seoul: Hongsŏnsa, 1979.

Kim Yŏng-jak. *Kan-matsu nashonarizumu no kenkyū* [A Study of Nationalism of Late Yi Korea]. Tokyo: Tokyo University Press, 1975.

Kim, Yung Chung. "Great Britain and Korea, 1883–1887." Ph.D. dissertation, Indiana University, 1965.

Kojong sidae-sa [History of Kojong's Era]. 6 vols. Seoul: Kuksa p'yŏnch'an wiwŏnhoe, 1967–70.

Ko Pyŏng-ik. "Mok In-dŏk ŭi hobinggwa kŭ paegyŏng" [Background of von Möllendorff's Employment]. *Chindan Hakbo* 25–27 (December 1964): 227–32.

———— [Koh Byong-ik]. "The Role of the Westerners Employed by the Korean Government in the Late Yi Dynasty." In *International Conference on the Problems of Modernization in Asia.* Seoul: Koryŏ taehakkyo Asea munje yŏn'guso [Asiatic Research Center of Korea University], 1965.

Korea, Ministry of Foreign Affairs. *Ku Hanmal oegyo munsŏ: Mi'guk kwan'gye p'yŏn* [Diplomatic Documents of the Late Yi Dynasty: American Correspondence]. Seoul: Tonga ch'ulp'ansa, 1960.

Korea Times

Korea Week

Kuehl, Walter F. *Dissertations in History, 1873–1970.* 2 vols. Lexington: University Press of Kentucky, 1965–72.

Ku Han'guk oegyo munsŏ: Aan [Diplomatic Documents of the Late Yi Dynasty: Russian Archives]. Seoul: Koryŏ taehakkyo Asea munje yŏn'guso [Asiatic Research Center of Korea University, comp.], 1965–70.

Ku Hanmal choyak hwich'an [Treaties of the Late Yi Dynasty]. Seoul: Kukhoe tosŏgwan, 1965.

Kwak, Tae-Hwan, John Chay, Soon Sung Cho, and Shannon McCune, eds. *U.S.–Korean Relations, 1882–1982*. Seoul: Kyungnam University Press, 1982.

Ladd, George Trumbull. *In Korea with Marquis Ito*. New York: Charles Scribner's Sons, 1908.

LaFeber, Walter. *The New Empire: An Interpretation of American Expansion, 1860–1898*. Ithaca: Cornell University Press, 1963.

Langer, William L. *The Diplomacy of Imperialism, 1890–1902*. New York: Alfred A. Knopf, 1935.

Lauterbach, Richard E. *History of the American Military Government in Korea*. Seoul: Kukche shinmun-sa, 1948.

Lee, Chong-Sik. *The Politics of Korean Nationalism*. Berkeley and Los Angeles: University of California Press, 1963.

Lee, Edmund J. *Lee of Virginia, 1842–1892*. Philadelphia: Edmund J. Lee, 1895.

Lee, Jung Young. "The American Missionary Movement in Korea, 1882–1945." Paper presented at the Association for Asian Studies Annual Meeting, Chicago, April 1982.

Lee, Yur-Bok. "American Policy toward Korea during the Sino-Japanese War of 1894–1895." *Journal of Social Sciences and Humanities* 43 (June 1976): 81–97.

———. *Diplomatic Relations between the United States and Korea, 1866–1887*. New York: Humanities Press, 1970.

———. *Establishment of a Korean Legation in the United States, 1887–1890: A Study of Conflict between Confucian World Order and Modern International Relations*, Illinois Papers in Asian Studies, vol. 3. Urbana: Center for Asian Studies, University of Illinois, 1983.

———. "P. G. von Möllendorff and the First Secret Russo-Korea Agreement of 1885." In *Proceedings of the Southwest Conference for Asian Studies*, pp. 90–107. New Orleans, 1980.

Lensen, George Alexander. *Balance of Intrigue: International Rivalry in Korea and Manchuria, 1884–1899*. 2 vols. Tallahassee: University Presses of Florida, 1982.

Lew, Young-ick. "American Advisers in Korea, 1885–1894: Anatomy of Failure." In Andrew C. Nahm, ed., *The United States and Korea: American-Korean Relations, 1866–1976*. Kalamazoo: Center for Korean Studies, Western Michigan University, 1979.

―――――. "The Shufeldt Treaty and Early Korean-American Interaction, 1882–1905." In Sung-joo Han, ed., *After One Hundred Years: Continuity and Change in Korean-American Relations.* Seoul: Koryŏ taehakkyo Asea munje yŏn'guso [Asiatic Research Center of Korea University], 1982.

Lin Ming-te. *Yüan Shih-k'ai yü Chao-hsien* [Yüan Shih-k'ai and Korea]. Taipei: The Institute of Modern History, Academia Sinica, 1970.

Livermore, Seward W. "American Naval Base Policy in the Far East, 1850–1914." *Pacific Historical Review* 13 (June 1944): 113–35.

Lo Kye-hyŏn. *Han'guk oegyosa yŏn'gu* [Studies on Korean Diplomatic History]. Seoul: Haemunsa, 1967.

McCormick, Thomas C. *China Market.* Chicago: Quadrangle Press, 1967.

McCune, George M., and John A. Harrison, eds. *Korean-American Relations: Documents Pertaining to the Far Eastern Diplomacy of the United States,* volume 1, *The Initial Period, 1883–1886.* Berkeley and Los Angeles: University of California Press, 1963.

McIntyre, W. D. "Anglo-American Rivalry in the Pacific." *Pacific Historical Review* 29 (November 1960): 361–77.

McKenzie, F. A. *Korea's Fight for Freedom.* New York: Fleming H. Revell, 1920.

MacKirdy, K. A. "The Fear of Intervention as a Factor in British Expansion." *Pacific Historical Review* 35 (May 1966): 123–39.

MacNair, Harvey F., and Donald F. Lach. *Modern Far Eastern International Relations.* 2nd ed., New York: Van Nostrand, 1955.

Malin, James C. *An Interpretation of Recent American History.* New York: Century, 1926.

Merli, Frank J., and Theodore A. Wilson. *Makers of American Diplomacy.* New York: Charles Scribner's Sons, 1974.

Michener, James A., and A. Grove Day. *Rascals in Paradise.* New York: Random House, 1957.

Minger, Ralph E. *William Howard Taft and United States Foreign Policy: The Apprenticeship Years, 1900–1908.* Urbana: University of Illinois Press, 1975.

Minutes and Reports of the Chōsen Mission of the Presbyterian Church in the U.S.A. Philadelphia: Presbyterian Foreign Mission Board, 1936.

Miyaje Setsurei. *Dōjidai shi* [History of the Same Period]. Tokyo: Iwanami shoten, 1950.

Moffett, Samuel H. "Missionaries Contributed to Korea." In *D.R.P.: The*

Official Bulletin of the Democratic Republican Party 10, no. 11 (November 1975): 19–20.

Möllendorff, Rosalie von. *P. G. von Möllendorff: Ein Lebensbild.* Leipzig: O. Harrassowitz, 1930.

Mommsen, W. J. *Theories of Imperialism.* New York: Random House, 1980.

Morrison, Elting E., John M. Blum, and Alfred D. Chandler, Jr., eds. *The Letters of Theodore Roosevelt.* 8 vols. Cambridge, Mass.: Harvard University Press, 1951–54.

Morse, Henry B. *The International Relations of the Chinese Empire.* London: Longmans Green, 1910.

Mun Il-p'yŏng. *Han-Mi osipnyŏnsa* [A Fifty-Year History of Korean-American Relations]. Seoul: Chongwangsa, 1945; Yi Kwang-rin, ed., reprint ed., Seoul: T'amgudang, 1975.

Mutsu Munemitsu. *Kenkenroku: A Diplomatic Record of the Sino-Japanese War, 1894–95.* Gordon Mark Berger, ed. and trans. Princeton: Princeton University Press, and Tokyo: Tokyo University Press, 1982.

———. *Kenkenroku* [Records of Turbulence—A Diplomatic Record of the Sino-Japanese War, 1894–1895]. Tokyo: Iwanami shoten, 1967.

Nahm, Andrew C. "American-Korean Relations, 1866–1976: An Overview." In Andrew C. Nahm, ed., *The United States and Korea: American-Korean Relations, 1866–1976.* Kalamazoo: Center for Korean Studies, Western Michigan University, 1979.

———. "Durham White Stevens and the Japanese Annexation of Korea." In Andrew C. Nahm, ed., *The United States and Korea: American-Korean Relations, 1866–1976.* Kalamazoo: Center for Korean Studies, Western Michigan University, 1979.

———. "U.S. Policy and the Japanese Annexation of Korea." In Tae-Hwan Kwak, John Chay, Soon Sung Cho, and Shannon McCune, eds., *U.S.-Korean Relations, 1882–1982.* Seoul: Kyungnam University Press, 1982.

Nelson, M. Frederick. *Korea and the Old Orders in Eastern Asia.* Baton Rouge: Louisiana State University Press, 1945; reprint ed., New York: Russell & Russell, 1967.

New York Daily Tribune

New York Times

Nichols, Roy F. *Advance Agents of American Destiny.* Philadelphia: University of Pennsylvania Press, 1956.

Noble, Harold J. "Korea and Her Relations with the United States before 1895." Ph.D. dissertation, University of California, 1931.

———. "The United States and Sino-Korean Relations, 1885–1887." *Pacific Historical Review* 2 (1933): 292–304.

Norman, E. Herbert. *Japan's Emergence as a Modern State.* New York: Institute of Pacific Relations, 1960.

Oh, Bonnie B. "John M. B. Sill." In Andrew C. Nahm, ed., *The United States and Korea: American-Korean Relations, 1866–1976.* Kalamazoo: Center for Korean Studies, Western Michigan University, 1979.

Oh, M. W. "The Two Visits of Reverend R. J. Thomas to Korea." *Transactions of the Royal Asiatic Society, Korea Branch* 22 (1933): 97–123.

Oh, Se Eung. "Dr. Philip Jaisohn's Reform Movement, 1896–1898." Ph.D. dissertation, American University, 1971.

Oliver, Robert T. "Arthur H. Vandenberg." *Quarterly Journal of Speech* 34, no. 3 (October 1948): 317–21.

———. *Syngman Rhee and American Involvement in Korea, 1942–1960.* Seoul: Panmun, 1978.

———. *Syngman Rhee: The Man behind the Myth.* New York: Dodd, Mead, 1955.

———. *Why War Came in Korea.* New York: Fordham University Press, 1950.

Oppert, Ernest. *A Forbidden Land.* New York: G. P. Putnam's Sons, 1880.

Paik, L. George. *The History of Protestant Missions in Korea, 1832–1910.* 2nd ed. Seoul: Yonsei University Press, 1971.

Pak Il-gŭn [Il-keun Park]. "China's Policy toward Korea, 1880–1884." *Journal of Social Sciences and Humanities,* no. 53 (June 1981): 45–77.

———. *Kŭndae Han-Mi oegyosa* [The Modern Diplomatic History of America and Korea]. Seoul: Pakusa, 1968.

———. *Mi'guk ŭi kae'guk chŏngch'aek kwa Han-Mi oegyo kwan'gye* [The American Open Door Policy and Korean-American Diplomatic Relations]. Seoul: Ilchogak, 1981.

Palais, James B. *Politics and Policy in Traditional Korea.* Cambridge, Mass.: Harvard University Press, 1975.

———. "Political Leadership in the Yi Dynasty." In Dae-sook Suh and Chae-jin Lee, eds., *Political Leadership in Korea.* Seattle and London: University of Washington Press, 1976.

Palmer, Spencer J. "American Gold Mining in Korea's Unsan District." *Pacific Historical Review* 31 (November 1962): 378–91.

———. ed. *Korean-American Relations: Documents Pertaining to the*

Far Eastern Diplomacy of the United States, volume 2, *The Period of Growing Influence, 1887–1895.* Berkeley and Los Angeles: University of California Press, 1963.

Paolino, Ernest N. *The Foundations of the American Empire: William Henry Seward and U.S. Foreign Policy.* Ithaca: Cornell University Press, 1973.

Patterson, Wayne. "Public Criticism versus Private Diplomacy in the Carter Human Rights Policy toward Korea." Unpublished paper, presented at 36th Annual Meeting of the Association for Asian Studies, Washington, D.C., March 23–25, 1984.

———. "Horace Allen and Korean Immigration to Hawaii." In Andrew C. Nahm, ed., *The United States and Korea: American-Korean Relations, 1866–1976.* Kalamazoo: Center for Korean Studies, Western Michigan University, 1979.

Paullin, Charles O. *Diplomatic Negotiations of American Naval Officers, 1778–1883.* Baltimore: Johns Hopkins University Press, 1912.

Plesur, Milton. *America's Outward Thrust.* DeKalb: Northern Illinois University Press, 1971.

Pletcher, David M. *The Anxious Years: American Foreign Relations under Garfield and Arthur.* Columbia: University of Missouri Press, 1963.

———. "Rhetoric and Empire." *Diplomatic History* 5 (Spring 1981): 93–105.

Pollard, Robert T. "America's Relations with Korea, 1882–1885." *Chinese Social and Political Science Review* 16 (October 1932): 425–71.

Presseisen, Ernest L. "Roots of Japanese Imperialism: A Memorandum of General LeGendre." *Journal of Modern History* 29, no. 2 (1957): 108–11.

Pringle, Henry F. *Theodore Roosevelt: A Biography.* New York: Harcourt, 1931.

Reeve, W. D. *The Republic of Korea: A Political and Economic Study.* London, New York, and Toronto: Oxford University Press, 1963.

Reischauer, Edwin O. "Back to Normalcy." *Foreign Policy* 20 (Fall 1975): 199–208.

———. *The United States and Japan.* 3rd ed., New York: Viking Press, 1965.

Reordan, Robert E. "The Role of George Clayton Foulk in the United States-Korean Relations, 1884–1887." Ph.D. dissertation, Fordham University, 1955.

Ro, Kwang Hai. "Power Politics in Korea and Its Impact on Korean Foreign and Domestic Affairs, 1882–1907." Ph.D. dissertation, University of Oklahoma, 1966.

Rockhill, W. W. *China's Intercourse with Korea from the XVth Century to 1895.* London: Luzac and Co., 1905.

_____. "Korea in Its Relations with China." *Journal of the American Oriental Society* 3 (1889): 1–33.

_____. *Notes on the Imperial Commission to Korea, 1890.* Shanghai, 1892.

_____. *Rockhill Manuscripts.* Harvard University.

_____. *Treaties and Conventions with or concerning China and Korea.* 2 vols. Washington, D.C.: Government Printing Office, 1904 and 1908.

Roosevelt, Theodore. *Roosevelt Manuscripts.* Washington, D.C., Library of Congress.

Rose, Lisle A. *After Yalta.* New York: Charles Scribner's Sons, 1973.

Sands, William Franklin. "Adventures of a Dictator." *Forum* 84, no. 4 (October 1930): 240–41, 252–56.

_____. "Dictator to an Emperor." *Forum* 84, no. 3 (September 1930): 140–41, 188–92.

_____. *Undiplomatic Memories: The Far East, 1896–1904.* New York: Whittlesley House, 1930.

San Francisco Chronicle

Scalapino, Robert A., and Chong-Sik Lee. *Communism in Korea.* 2 vols. Berkeley: University of California Press, 1972.

Schiffman, James R. "Korean Protests, Worst in Chun's Rule, Take an Anti-American Undercurrent." *Wall Street Journal,* December 8, 1983.

Schley, W. W. "Our Navy in Korea." *Harper's Weekly* 38 (August 1894): 779–84.

Sheehan, D., and H. C. Syrett. *Essays in American Historiography.* New York: Columbia University Press, 1960.

Shippe, L. B. "Thomas Francis Bayard." In Samuel Flagg Bemis, et al., eds., *The American Secretaries of State and Their Diplomacy.* Vol. 8. New York: Alfred A. Knopf, 1927–29.

Shufeldt, Robert W. *Address Delivered before the African Colonization Society.* Washington, D.C., 1877.

_____. "Corea's Trouble." *San Francisco Chronicle,* October 30, 1887.

_____. *Relation of the Navy to the Commerce of the United States.* Washington, D.C., 1878.

————. *Shufeldt Manuscripts.* Washington, D.C., Library of Congress.

Shulman, Frank L. *Doctoral Dissertations on Japan and Korea, 1969–1979.* Seattle: University of Washington Press, 1982.

Sill, John M. B. *Sill Manuscripts.* University of Michigan.

Sin Ki-sŏk. *Hanmal oegyosa yŏn'gu* [Studies on the Diplomatic History of the Late Yi Dynasty]. Seoul: Ilchogak, 1967.

Smith, Shirley. "John M. B. Sill." In *Michigan and the Cleveland Era.* Ann Arbor: University of Michigan Press, 1948.

Son In-ju. "Han'guk kŭndae hakkyo ŭi sŏngnip kwajŏng" [History of the Development of Korea's Modern Schools]. In *Yi Hae-nam paksa hwangap kinyŏm sahak nonch'ong* [Essays in Commemoration of the 61st Birthday of Dr. Yi Hae-nam]. Seoul: Ilchogak, 1970.

Song Pyŏng-gi. "Sipgu segimal ŭi yŏnmiron sosŏl: Yi Hong-chang ŭi milhamŭ chungsim ŭro" [An Introduction to the Korean Alliance with America in the Late Nineteenth Century: Centering on Li Hung-chang's Confidential Letters]. *Sahakchi* 9 (November 1975): 61–88.

Spence, Jonathan. *To Change China: Western Advisors in China, 1620–1960.* New York: Little, Brown, 1969.

Swartout, Robert R., Jr. *Mandarins, Gunboats, and Power Politics: Owen Nickerson Denny and the International Rivalries in Korea,* Asian Studies at Hawaii, no. 25. Honolulu: University Press of Hawaii, 1980.

————. "United States Ministers to Korea, 1882–1905: The Loss of American Innocence." *Transactions of the Royal Asiatic Society, Korean Branch* 57 (1982): 41–52.

————, ed. *An American Adviser in Late Yi Korea: The Letters of Owen Nickerson Denny.* University: University of Alabama Press, 1984.

Tabohashi Kiyoshi. *Kindai Nissen kankei no kenkyū* [A Study of Modern Japanese-Korean Relations]. 2 vols. Keijō: Chōsen sōtokufu, 1940.

Tansill, Charles C. *The Foreign Policy of Thomas F. Bayard, 1885–1897.* New York: Fordham University Press, 1940.

Tewksbury, Donald G. *Source Materials on Korean Politics and Ideology.* New York: Institute of Pacific Relations, 1950.

Thompson, Sandra. "Filibustering to Formosa: General Charles LeGendre and the Japanese." *Pacific Historical Review* 40, no. 4 (November 1971): 442–56.

Treat, Payson J. "China and Korea, 1885–1894." *Political Science Quarterly* 49 (December 1934): 506–43.

_____. *Diplomatic Relations between the United States and Japan, 1853–1905*. 3 vols. Stanford: Stanford University Press, 1932–38.

Truman, Harry S. *Memoirs*. New York: Doubleday, 1956.

Tsungli Yamen. *Chao-hsien tang* [Korean Archives]. Taipei: Institute of Modern History, Academia Sinica.

Tyler, Alice F. *The Foreign Policy of James G. Blaine*. Minneapolis: University of Minnesota Press, 1927.

United Nations Document A/C/1/230 (October 29, 1947).

United States Congress. *Congressional Record*, vol. 58, 1919.

_____. Senate Subcommittee on U.S. Security Agreements and Commitments Abroad of the Committee on Foreign Relations. *United States Security and Commitments Abroad: Republic of Korea*. Washington, D.C.: Government Printing Office, 1970.

United States, Department of State. *Bulletin*, October 21, 1945.

_____. *Country Reports on Human Rights Practices, Korea*. Washington, D.C.: Government Printing Office, 1981.

_____. *Despatches from United States Minister to China, 1843–1906*. File microcopies of records in the National Archives, Washington, D.C., no. 92.

_____. *Despatches from United States Minister to Japan, 1885–1906*. File microcopies of records in the National Archives, Washington, D.C., no. 133.

_____. *Despatches from United States Minister to Korea, 1883–1905*. File microcopies of records in the National Archives, Washington, D.C., no. 134.

_____. *Diplomatic Instructions of the Department of State, 1801–1906: China*. File microcopies of records in the National Archives, Washington, D.C., no. 77.

_____. *Diplomatic Instructions of the Department of State, 1801–1906: Japan*. File microcopies of records in the National Archives, Washington, D.C., no. 77.

_____. *Diplomatic Instructions of the Department of State, 1801–1906: Korea*. File microcopies of records in the National Archives, Washington, D.C., no. 77.

_____. *A History of United States–Korean Relations, 1834–1962*. Washington, D.C.: Government Printing Office, 1962.

_____. *Notes* from Korean legation in the United States to the Department of State, 1883–1906. File microcopies of records in the National Archives, Washington, D.C., no. 166.

_____. *Papers Relating to the Foreign Relations of the United States, 1867–1945.*

_____. *President Ford's Pacific Doctrine,* Department of State news release, December 7, 1975.

_____. *Report on Korea.* Washington, D.C.: Government Printing Office, 1979.

_____. *The Secretary of State Speech,* Department of State news release, November 24, 1975.

_____. *Treaties and Conventions Concluded by the United States of America since July 4, 1776.* Washington, D.C.: Government Printing Office, 1889.

_____. *United States Chiefs of Mission, 1778–1982.* Washington, D.C.: Government Printing Office, 1983.

United States Embassy, Seoul. *Economic Trends Report,* January 12, 1981.

U.S. News and World Report

Varg, Paul A. *Open Door Diplomat: The Life of W. W. Rockhill.* Urbana: University of Illinois Press, 1952.

Vaya, Count Vay de and Luskod. *Empires and Emperors of Russia, China, Korea, and Japan.* New York: E. P. Dutton, 1906.

Vevier, Charles. "The Collins Overland Line." *Pacific Historical Review* 28 (August 1959): 237–53.

Washington Post

Weems, Clarence N. "The Korean Reform and Independence Movement, 1881–1898." Ph.D. dissertation, Columbia University, 1954.

Weinert, Richard P. "The Original KMAG."*Military Review* (June 1965): 93–99.

West, Richard W., Jr. *Admirals of American Empire.* Indianapolis: Bobbs Merrill, 1948.

Weston, Robin F. *Racism in U.S. Imperialism.* Columbia: University of South Carolina Press, 1972.

White, John A. *The Diplomacy of the Russo-Japanese War.* Princeton: Princeton University Press, 1964.

Who Was Who in America, 1897–1942. Chicago: Marquis, 1943.

Wilkie, Wendell. *One World.* New York: Pocket Books, 1943.

Williams, S. Wells. *The History of China.* London: Sampson, Low, 1897.

Williams, William Appleman. *The Tragedy of American Diplomacy.* Cleveland: World, 1959.

Wright, Mary C. "The Adaptability of Ch'ing Diplomacy: The Case of Korea." *Journal of Asian Studies* 17 (May 1958): 363–81.

Yi Kwang-rin [Lee, Kwang-rin]. "Early Relations: Conflicting Images." Academy of Korean Studies and the Wilson Center, ed. In *Reflections on a Century of United States–Korean Relations: Conference Papers*. Lanham, N.Y., and London: University Press of America, 1983.
———. *Han'guk kaehwasa yŏn'gu* [A Study on the History of Enlightenment in Korea]. Seoul: Ilchogak, 1969.
Yi Sŏn-gŭn. *Han'guksa: Ch'oegŭnse-p'yŏn* [History of Korea: The Most Recent Period]. Seoul: Ŭryu munhwasa, 1964.
———. *Han'guksa: Hyŏndae-p'yŏn* [History of Korea: The Modern Era]. Seoul: Ŭryu munhwasa, 1964.
———. "Kyŏngjin susinsa Kim Hong-jip kwa Hwang Chun-hŏn jŏ Chosŏn ch'aeknyak e kwanhan chae-kŏmt'o" [Reevaluation of Susinsa Kim Hong-jip and Hwang Chun-hŏn's "A Policy for Korea"]. *Tonga nonch'ong* 1 (1963): 254–59.
Yi Wŏn-sun. "Hanmal Cheju-do t'ongŏ munje ilgo" [A Study of Fishery Problems in Cheju Island during the Late Yi Dynasty]. *Yŏksa kyoyuk* 10 (December 1967): 142–71.
Young, Marilyn B. "American Expansion, 1870–1900." In Barton J. Bernstein, ed., *Towards a New Past*. New York: Pantheon, 1968.
Yun Ch'i-ho. *Yun Ch'i-ho Ilgi* [Diary]. 5 vols. Seoul: Kuksa p'yŏnch'an wiwŏnhoe, 1973–75.

Contributors

Hilary Conroy, Co-Chairperson of the International Relations and East Asian Studies Program at the University of Pennsylvania, has published several books and numerous articles. He is the author of *The Japanese Frontier in Hawaii* (University of California Press, 1953) and *The Japanese Seizure of Korea* (University of Pennsylvania Press, 1960), and co-editor of *Japan Examined* (University of Hawaii Press, 1983). Various articles or book reviews of his have appeared in the *Journal of Asian Studies, American Historical Review, Pacific Historical Review,* and in many other academic journals.

Fred Harvey Harrington is President Emeritus at the University of Wisconsin. His works include *God, Mammon, and the Japanese* (University of Wisconsin Press, 1944) and *Fighting Politician* (University of Pennsylvania Press, 1948). He has published articles in the *Mississippi Valley Historical Review* (now the *Journal of American History*) and other scholarly journals and is now preparing a book on the late Indira Gandhi's 1975–77 "emergency" in India.

Wi Jo Kang is the endowed Chair Professor of Mission at Wartburg Theological Seminary, as well as the author of *Christian Presence in Japan* (Seibunsha, 1981), *Religion and Politics in Korea under the Japanese Rule* (Christian Literature Society, 1977), and many articles for religious journals. He is presently revising a manuscript, "Christianity and Politics in Modern Korea," which is to be published as a book.

Tae-Hwan Kwak, Professor of Political Science at Eastern Kentucky University, is co-editor of and contributor to several books, which includes *Problems of Korean Unification* (Research Center for Peace and Unification, 1976). He has published articles in such journals as *Asian Profile* and *Korean Journal of International Studies.* He is currently conducting research on the problems pertaining to reunification of Korea.

Yur-Bok Lee, Professor of History at North Dakota State University, has written *Diplomatic Relations between the United States and Korea* (Humanities Press, 1970) and *Establishment of a Korean Lega-*

182

tion in the United States (Center for Asian Studies of the University of Illinois, 1983). Various articles or book reviews of his are published in the *Journal of Asian Studies, Journal of Social Sciences and Humanities,* and *American Historical Review.* He is completing another book-size manuscript, "Great Power Intervention in Korea and the Involvement of Paul Georg von Möllendorff."

Robert T. Oliver, Professor Emeritus of Pennsylvania State University, served for twenty years as an adviser to President Syngman Rhee on South Korea's international relations. He has written half a dozen books and numerous articles on Korea, including *Why War Came in Korea* (Fordham University Press, 1950), *Syngman Rhee* (Dodd, Mead, 1955), and *Syngman Rhee and American Involvement in Korea* (Panmun, 1978).

Wayne Patterson, Associate Professor of History at St. Norbert College, is co-author of *The Koreans in America* (Lerner, 1977) and co-editor of *Japan in Transition* (Associated University Presses, 1984) and *The Koreans in America, 1882–1974* (Oceana, 1974). Various articles or book reviews of his are published in *Diplomatic History, Pacific Affairs, Asian Forum, Korean Studies,* and the *Annals of the American Academy of Political and Social Sciences.* He is currently completing a book on the immigration of Koreans to the United States at the turn of the century.

Index

31–34, 45, 55; and American investment in Korea, 35, 37, 39–40, 61–65; and missionaries, 38–39, 49, 54

Kŏmundo. *See* Port Hamilton

Korea: relations with the United States, 1–11 passim, 13, 25–26, 34–38, 40–45, 53, 60–61, 68, 161 (n. 31); traditional ties to China, 3, 15–20, 37, 41, 52, 56, 60, 149 (n. 60); and the Japanese colonial government, 7, 46, 54, 57, 61, 68–69, 71–72, 78–79, 84–85; sovereignty of, 15–18, 21, 41, 56–57, 68, 71, 129 (n. 13), 149–50 (n. 60). *See also* Kojong, King and Emperor

"Koreagate," 119, 121

Korean-American (Shufeldt or Chemulp'o) Treaty, 13, 15–17, 53–54, 57, 61; and the good-offices clause, 2, 19–22, 24–26, 40, 42, 57, 61, 152 (n. 75)

Korean Armistice, 105

Korean Communists, 90, 94–95

Korean independence, 3, 6, 22, 25, 55–57, 62, 67, 69–70, 87–88, 90–91, 97; "in due course," 91. *See also* Korean nationalist movement; Trusteeship

Korean-Japanese (Kwanghwa) Treaty, 13, 16–17, 27

Korean-Japanese Protectorate Treaty, 68

Korean nationalist movement, 6, 89

Korean Provisional Government (KPG), 89, 94, 97, 99, 101

Korean War (1950–53), 8–10, 103–4, 108

Kwangju Uprising (1980), 120, 125

LeGendre, Charles W., 32–33, 148 (n. 53)

Li Hung-chang, 13, 17–18, 31–32, 52, 65–66

Limb, Colonel Ben C., 98

Low, Frederick F., 50, 144 (nn. 17, 25), 145 (n. 31)

MacArthur, General Douglas, 92, 103–4

Marshall, George, 99

Merrill, Henry F., 32

Min (Queen), 12, 39; murdered, 23, 44, 66

Min Yŏng-ch'an, 26

Minami Jiro, 84

Missionaries, 38–40, 53–54, 65; sympathetic to Korean independence, 6–7, 38, 68–70, 77; policies of, 68, 70–71; and clashes with Japanese, 69, 72, 75–77, 83–85. *See also* Conspiracy Case; Independence movement

Miura Gorō, 44, 66

Möllendorff, Paul Georg von, 31–32, 45

Morgan, Edwin V., 25–26, 38, 70

Morse, James R., 65

Moscow Conference, 92–93, 99

Mutual Security Pact (1954), 105, 108

Nationalists. *See* Korean nationalist movement

Neutrality of Korea, 23–25

Nixon, Richard M., 10, 105, 109, 112

North Atlantic Treaty Organization (NATO), 105, 109

North Korea, 2, 8, 10, 94, 100–3, 113–19, 124–25. *See also* Kim Il-sung (Kim Il-sŏng)

Olney, Robert, 23, 58

Open Door policy, 23, 36–37, 47

Pacific Doctrine (1975), 112. *See also* Ford, Gerald R.

Pacific War, 8, 88

Pacific War Council, 88